Pushback!
The Action Manual, Lite

by New Ideas

PUSHBACK!

THE ACTION MANUAL, LITE

by New Ideas

the small life company, inc.

Table of Contents

Introduction to the Action Manual, Lite

1. Parallel Worlds.

We have two groups of people living in parallel worlds in America. The "Life Is Sweet" group is made up of a small set of a financial elite and other self-interested citizens. For them, life is is about "As Good As It Gets."

The second is the "Grind It out" group of multi-millions of ordinary Americans, like most of us. They are the so-called "little people" whose social world lives are characterized mostly by insecurity, frustration, anger, and broken spirits.

Over the past 30 years or so, things have been getting steadily worse for the little people. Many of them believe that the stark differences between the two groups in economic, political, social status, and outcomes is unfair. They feel the system is rigged against them. However, they haven't been able to do much of anything about it. They feel helpless and hopeless.

2. The Action Manual.

Doing something about this unfair and rigged situation is what this Action Manual is about. It explains:

-why we have this parallel world situation in America

-that we have 18th-Century governance and social relations systems which are not appropriate for our times

-that vast progress has been made in nearly all areas of American life *except* for how we govern ourselves and relate to one another

-why the many prior major social change efforts have failed

-and, why the right time is now for an updated and improved social world, what that society can look like, and how we can get it.

3. Why is now different?

-the little people have way more information about the nature of our social world than ever before and have learned about social change from decades of experience

-there are vast new technological tools like the Internet, Web 2.0 databases, social media, mobile devices and more for people who are willing to work for change which make information distribution, communications, and organization much more potent than ever before

-there *have* been prior successful historical examples of change, for example, the civil rights and gender rights movements, which provide models of sorts for how merely new ways of seeing and thinking can make for major social changes

-there is a significantly large consensus among the little people of needs for security, **balance** between private and public interests, human **meanings**, and **respect** for the "small life" (BMR), and for smarter governance and social relations

4. What is needed now.

A new theoretically-sound vision and a fresh practical plan of change, together with existing resources and political will, can work to catalyze citizen action for major social change

- new ways of seeing and thinking about economics, politics, and social life more relevant to 21st-Century realities may guide fair-minded and progressive people to affect great changes in a just allocation of economic value, political influence, and social status

-a new social ethos containing concepts of a collective interest, rationality, and fairness; new public values; and greater reliance on professional expertise, science, and reason may be the key to convincing people of the need and possibility of significant social change

-a plan involving a unified set of activist people and groups covering a wide range of political attitudes and positions under a *single* brand having **focus, accessibility**, and **ease** of participation may be sufficient in "pushing back" the individualist/capitalist ethos which dominates us now.

5. The vision and a plan together form a *National Character Program*. That program includes:

-a new social ethos with a new set of public values

-a set of national councils representing collective perspective, fairness, rationality, inclusiveness, and professional governance

-the formation of a national collective identity– an American "Team Player" group--as an alternative to the "solo" individuals, special interests, and egos which now dominate American society

-the creation of a shadow government of sorts, as a complement to existing legal government and the influence of Big Business, including participation by the little people themselves

-a deepened respect for reason, science, and facts, and professionalism in both formal and informal institutions

-a sense that the time is right now for the little people to get their due. That means a pushback of individualism/capitalism and the creation of an advanced 21st-Century American society.

6. Chapter descriptions:

Chapter 1- An overview of a vision and a plan as a story outline of why and how the little people organize into American Team Players. They promote the formation of a new social ethos and a sense of public citizenship, a brain and governance, and a shadow government. And, they demand balance, meaning, and respect for everyone, regardless of relative social status. Readers are challenged to flesh out and complete the story.

Chapter 2-A description of the Characters of the story, primarily, private self-interested persons and collectively-minded public citizens.

Chapter 3-A description of the Setting of the story, which is our 18th-Century governance and social systems dominated by ideologies of individualism and capitalism.

Chapter 4 -The Back Story of prior failed reform efforts to change the lives of multimillions of little people Americans.

Chapter 5-A description of the Functions of the program

Chapter 6-A description and explanation of Public Values vs. Private ones

Chapter 7-A description of What Do We Need Now-including a set of specific economic, political, and social changes

Chapter 8-A description of the Program itself – its structure and processes

Chapter 9-An explanation of What's Next. That includes a description of how readers can write the rest of the story and what kind of people are needed to implement the plan, together with checklists and a timeline of what has to be done and when.

In essence, the book is a story outline challenging readers to supply the detail and to write their own ending. It is a story of how the little people can obtain balance, meaning, and respect (BMR) and establish Smart governance and social relations for themselves and future generations.

Just participating in the program, regardless of its success or not, will be a meaningful experience for many readers eager to have a fighting chance for rights and dignity. They will have pride in their efforts in participating in a Grand Adventure.

Note: Sooner or later, readers will realize that no one ("New Ideas" is a pseudonym) has claimed authorship of this book. That, of course, is unusual and a bit strange. The anonymity is intended, as the focus has to be on the *story*. And, *you readers* are the true focus of the rest of the story as you are expected to write most of it in any case. Let's keep it at that.

Also, there is an associated "Full" version of this book called The Action Manual. Instead of having mere talking points, as contained here in theLite version, the full version has extensive explanations of all of the talking points together with examples and illustrations. It is recommended that those sincerely interested in understanding the National Character Program in all of its richness, complexity, and elegance read that book first.

The Vision and the Plan

1. A new social ethos with a new set of public values

2. A set of informal National Councils representing a collective perspective and collective fairness

3. The Councils:
> National
> Policy and Problem Solving
> Planning
> Information
> Support
> Local
>
> The National University

4. The American Team, Comprised of Public Citizens, balancing private and public (Collective) Interests

5. The Shadow Government pushing back Individualism/Capitalism

6. Smart Governance and Professionalism

Chapter 1-The Story Outline

The American Individualist/Capitalist System

Multimillions of ordinary American people (quiet Marys and Johns) lost jobs, homes, pensions, and more for no reasons of their own during the Great Recession of 2008. A small set of aggressive, self-interested people responsible for the financial crisis either made money from it or got bailouts from the taxpayers for their own losses. That was just the latest example of how a private citizen elite exploited the little people for their own self-interests.

Let's face it, hard-core capitalism is *really* the American way. There is an almost unrecognized fundamental conflict between private vs. public citizenship where private citizens emphasize individualism and capitalism and public citizens emphasize a balance of interests, human meanings, and respect for doing the best that they can in their social lives. The aggressive and selfish get regularly rewarded; the ordinary Marys and Johns don't exploit anybody but regularly get exploited and harmed just trying to do the right thing for their families and the communities they live in.

A lot of people feel that this is not right. This book presents a *story outline* of how this sorry situation gets fixed. The book is a challenge to readers. It is an *Action Manual* to inspire and guide ordinary people to pushback on private citizens and the financial elite to obtain not only balance, meaning, and respect (BMR) but to update and smarten American governance and social relations. (We haven't updated in those elements much since the 18th-Century.)

American society is deeply infused with an ideology of individualism and capitalism. It is dominated by a relatively small set of self-interested, aggressive, and willful people, which includes special interests and much of Big Business. They make up an elite.

The individualist/capitalist ideology results in an unbalanced system which provides overwhelming incentives for self-interested behavior while penalizing public interested ones. It has principles creating a structural imperative for everyone to be a competitive capitalist whether they want to or not. The system forces people to become winners or losers, and the great majority turn out to be losers. The system has no respect for the inevitable economic losers or for the little people in general. From the system's point of view, it's either succeed under the "rules of the game" or die. Hard work, good intentions, and best efforts in themselves mean nothing to it.

This system is also a heartless one which disregards social and human meanings. It insists on producing a population only of consumers and workers. No other social roles are important for it, even those of family, church, and community. The system imposes itself upon everyone all of the time. It justifies the most heartless and uncivil behaviors. After all—"Business Is Business!"

The individualist/capitalist ideology has resulted in a rigged system favoring only a small percentage of the population–the elite. Despite what the elite tells us, this is *not* a natural state of affairs. It has no theoretical components of what most Americans want (consciously or not)--a sense of a public good, collective fairness, and respect for the humanity of people.

The logic of this ideology makes the *system itself* fundamentally more important than the people who participate in it (or *for* it.) For the most part, this system results in a stressed population–insecure, distrustful, calculating, and cynical. Many people become alienated from their social lives. Clearly, this environment is not good for most people!

A great many fair-minded and right-minded people, however, believe that a quality, healthy society requires a balancing of private and public interests, space for human meanings, and respect for everyone who is trying to be the best that they can be. They want America to be that kind of society.

Politics and Government

Despite being a liberal democracy, voting numbers don't matter very much. The vast majority of little people rarely get the benefits of elections, policymaking, or governance in general. Self-interested private citizens and special interests dominate because they have the focus, intensity, and resources suitable for dominating our outmoded political processes.

Much of what happens in the political world is *theater*, that is, playacting, bluster, and pretending that even ordinary folks have meaningful roles to play. That theater hides the fact that despite frequent elections and such our political processes are perpetually dominated by an elite having short-term, self-interested motivations. Many of the little people know what their true status situations are but feel mostly helpless and sometimes hopeless. The losers, as well as everybody else, are subject to the rigged "Rules of the Game," and that game is competitive individualism and capitalism, favoring the elite.

Most of us have been taught that our governmental system was designed to protect the little people but it doesn't. It was supposedly meant to protect all of us from the worst traits of humanity and to enforce a common good. The historical reality is that the most active and vocal of the little people and even popular political personalities have been unable to enforce those ideals and it isn't even *possible* for anyone to do so, given the elite doesn't want it to happen.

Even though our traditional political theory says otherwise, our (18th-Century) government is mostly an instrument of manipulation and control used by the elite *against* the little people.

Old Ideas

 Our political system is an *18th-Century* system well out of place in contemporary times. There is no institution representing collective America. There is little or no imperative for collective perspective or rationality. The imperatives of the system reward intensity, focus, and wealth in politics as well as economics, and those who have it dominate, even over substantial majorities. We have an excessive openness in our government institutions which allows private citizens and special interests to "pay" their way inside to get at officials and political processes to assert overwhelming influence, mostly out of public view.

We are living under *really* old governance ideas. Our traditional principles of governance may have worked well under different facts and a different environment when individualism made more sense. In the 18th-Century, an emphasis on individualism, limited federal jurisdiction, diffusion of power, and an absence of a collective perspective and planning capabilities may have fit the mostly parochial social environment. That's when many people were self-sustaining farmers, there was little social interaction, and nobody knew much about anybody else in the world or had to deal with them.

But not now. 230-plus years later, we have a vastly changed world. We have advanced communications, transportation, and management systems; globalism; mega-cities; and more; all of which makes the individualism concept much less relevant for modern times. It is plain that the old ways of doing things are not working for most people.

We Need New Ideas.

We've had *some* very modest updating of our political world, including the New Deal programs and expanded federal jurisdiction in the 1930's and 60's. Nevertheless, we've had minimal political and social progress in *over 200 years* even in the midst of tremendous objective progress in nearly all other areas. The main problem is that there is no official person or *any* institution in American society in a position and with the incentives and authority to respond to modern needs.

A quality, modern government has these traits: a collective perspective and rationality; an emphasis on a common good; respect for science, reason, and facts; professionalism and trustworthiness; and a capability for medium to long-term planning; among others.

Our society has no collective perspective nor a "brain," of any sorts. That means we have no institutions representing *Americans as a whole.* We have only individuals and special interests who care only for themselves. We can't coordinate the disparate parts of society, we can't act rationally, and we lack medium to long-term planning functions. These flaws (and others) result in chronic waste and inefficiency, severely dysfunctional governance, lack of trust in institutions, and a cynical populace. No wonder we have a strong antigovernment attitude among many citizens.

Congress and the Presidency

We can't rely on Congress to have a collective perspective because it is designed to represent geographic regions (each with their own elites and special interests.) Its incentives are *against* a collective perspective and it is essentially "owned" anyway by Big Business and special interests. Neither can we rely on the President to enforce the principles of a collective or a brain. The President has truly limited powers, is beholden to campaign supporters (the elite, mostly), and subservient to the demands of the Big Business elite which dominates the economy, political processes, and even cultural matters. In fact, according to some political analysts, the government in general is essentially a sock puppet for Big Business. So much for "Government by the people, for the people"!

Social Habit

We are also burdened by the weight of social habit. We are still relying on 230+-year-old governmental institutions and resist even modest changes. Even in the Internet age, for example, with vastly advanced communications and management systems we still have *multi-thousands* of separate governmental bodies all with their own separate little jurisdictions, separate staffs, separate processes and budgets. (Where is the efficiency in that!?)

We Are Sick Of What We Have Become

For a nation which likes to call itself the "World's Greatest," we have fallen behind many countries in all kinds of areas, including a metric little thought of here, the "Happiness Index." Instead of becoming more friendly towards and tolerant of others, we have become more hateful and intolerant. Most people have no balance, meaning, nor respect in their lives nor experience a smart governance system. In any case, we are underachieving and our governance and social relationship systems are archaic.

Our society has a significant lack of economic justice, a collective perspective, class fairness, collective rationality, professionalism, efficiency, statesmanship, good social character, and even social decency. Millions of Americans are haunted by financial insecurity, political impotence, and worse. Most fair-minded people consider this situation as a disgrace and an embarrassment.

Prior Fixes

There have been efforts to fix this situation before. We've tried electing new parties and new governmental representatives, tried all kinds of legal structural reforms, and offered up prayers for magical new leadership. In the past century or so, we've had some trust-busting reforms, privately-founded large industrial unions, and experienced the Tea Party and Occupy Wall Street protests, but nothing permanently significant has come from *any* of these things.

However, there have been some "anti-ignorance" and anti-social habit movements, like the civil rights and feminist movements, which *have* been mostly successful. There are some lessons to be learned from them (see below.) But all of the *anti-economic injustice* movements have been near total failures. Even the vigorous labor movement of the 1930's through 70's, which was instrumental in creating the American middle class and in supporting the creation of much of our social safety net (among other progressive matters), has mostly been eviscerated by an elite counteroffensive and is now seriously weakened.

The elite have developed strategies to deal with all of those potential challenges to their dominance. They have come up with symbolic legislation, encouraged an electoral theater strategy of "rotating elites," and consistently offered to the little people the promise of "Change!" for *every* new election cycle. For the most part, the little people have either been consistently fooled or stymied.

Maybe Humans Can't Change

Clearly, there has been a giant absence of "subject" progress (i.e., how *people* govern ourselves and relate to each other) versus "object" (i.e., material things) progress, as in the medical sciences, engineering, computers, communications technology, etc. where progress has been tremendous.

For skeptics, like the Classical Conservatives, we *can't* improve human nature. It is what it is. They believe that people will always be selfish, aggressive, competitive, and otherwise flawed. They will rarely get along ever, except maybe in small tribal-like environments. For some theorists, the messy liberal democracy status quo we have now may be as good as it gets.

On the other hand, progressives and optimists, like the Classical Liberals, perceive some important advances in society over the centuries. As a whole, we are more educated; experience much more interaction globally and in virtual worlds; have moderated tribal attitudes somewhat; and formed advanced institutions like the United Nations, the European Union, and multi-lateral trade and cultural organizations. They believe more changes can come from more education, more interaction, use of advanced technology, and an *advanced social mindset*. An advanced social mindset means new ideas of governance and social relations. It could mean a new vision of a modern society and a practical plan to accomplish it, as proposed in this book.

The Start of a New Social Movement

There certainly is a lot of clamor by a lot of the little people for change. However, there is no plausibly effective plan being offered now by anyone. What is needed is a new social movement. What is needed is a realistic vision and a practical plan together with sufficient will, resources, and persistence. (The will and resources, anyway, seem to be there now.)

One of the components of an advanced society is a pushback of capitalism. We need to pushback to balance private and public interests, make space for human meanings, and obtain respect for all of the little people. For a number of important reasons, we are not going to eliminate capitalism so we must *work around* it. That is a necessary part of a coherent theoretical vision of an advanced society.

There are good reasons to believe that we *can* pushback capitalism. We have new information, tools, organizational abilities, and a historical set of models including the civil rights and feminist movements which show that a mindset-based movement *can* be successful. We can change the prevailing private citizen attitude of individualism to one of a *balance* of private and public interests. But, that is only a start.

Let's say we come up with a program which offers a new social ethos of the balancing of private and public interests; requires our institutions and businesses to recognize the humanity of their citizens, workers, and consumers; and offers respect and rewards for people achieving the best they can do regardless of their social status. Let's add a set of new public values, greater reliance on new science and technologies, permanent social conditioning designed to offer people accessible guidance to improving themselves and their communities, and more. This is becoming a comprehensive, practical plan. It will be a new narrative for the "American" nation and especially for the little people.

We may be able to inspire people to write this story with narratives of a new society. Getting the participation of many of the little people in a smart and open-ended program may open up creativity and productivity of millions of people who have been long repressed and neglected. We need to inform, convince, and inspire people of the real likelihood of significant change.

The program being offered here is an interactive story and a real-time experiment in social change. It offers nearly everyone an opportunity to participate in whatever way they choose towards creation of a program of change—the National Character Program.

The National Character Program

A New Social Ethos - Balance, Meaning, Respect, and Smart governance and social relations

A New Set of Public Values

– Collective fairness
– Trustworthiness in governance, business, and society
– Pride in oneself regardless of status
– Economic efficiency and meaning from a collective's perspective
– Enhanced respect for reason and science
– Consideration of multiple perspectives
– Humility in social engineering
– Insistence on quality of character
– Tolerance for trivial differences
- Inclusiveness

The Shadow Government

The National Council

The Brain

The Policy and Problem-Solving Council	The Planning Council	The Information Council	The Support Council	The Local Council

The American Team Players

The National University

The National Character Program

The program contains a theoretically-sound vision and a practical plan of organization. It is a paradigm, i.e., a new way of seeing and thinking about economic, political, and social matters. It contains a new social ethos of balance, meaning, and respect, together with smart governance and social relations. It offers a new set of public values, an informal "shadow" government run by the little people themselves, a formal set of six national councils representing a collective perspective and a brain in governance, an academic program to develop new leaders, and a new inclusive social category of Team Players acting as an American collective.

The most important component of the program is its set of public values. They include BMR, collective fairness, trustworthiness in government and the private sector, good social character, economic efficiency from a collective's perspective, and more. These values are likely to be shared by most people regardless of political attitudes. They balance both (capitalist) system needs and human needs. They offer a component of human meaning in both economic and political affairs. They imply a healthy respect for multiple perspectives and empathy and humility about social engineering

The program is not about specific policy contents but about problem-solving. It is a distinct *approach* to problem solving emphasizing a collective's perspective and reliance upon professional expertise and resources. If the approach itself is good it ought to equate eventually to good policy, good governance, and more harmonious social relations.

The plan involves pushback, not replacement of capitalism. It shows how to construct a shadow government to monitor and influence legal government and Big Business, especially by an activist Local Council. It explains how and why rewards and conditioning programs may lead to better citizens. It promotes templates of roles and behaviors designed by fair-minded experts for all kinds of social matters to make life *easier* for most people. (So many people would be absolutely thrilled to be able to live an easier life!) And, it encourages the formation of a Team Player social group designed to eliminate or minimize the trivial differences which create unnecessary friction among social groups of all kinds.

Conservative, Liberal, and Radical

The Program is both conservative, liberal and radical at the same time. It is conservative in that it doesn't envision a replacement of an entire system (capitalism) but only a *complementary* social ethos and informal governance. It emphasizes improving and modernizing what we have and not tearing down or destroying anything. It emphasizes personal values and individual action. It envisions a large space for spiritual and human life meanings regardless of system imperatives. It accepts the flaws of humanity and the limitations of social engineering.

It is liberal in that it envisions an active role of government and ordinary people in both formal and informal governance. (Informal governance will be by the shadow government organized and run by the little people.) It believes that the consistent application of science and reason can greatly aid problem-solving. It emphasizes social inclusiveness and and builds upon what it sees as the goodness and potential of all people.

It is radical in its concept of *dual citizen* attitude involving balancing of private and public interests. It offers a new balanced set of rules of the game, so to speak, involving collective rationality. It offers new structural checks and balances on both government and Big Business. It anticipates that new technology will empower the little people like they've never been before. It implements "building up" strategies for both society and for individuals. And, it provides for a set of permanent social conditioning programs using templates and more.

An *Action* Manual

This book is an *action* manual. While it offers a new theoretical paradigm of thinking and seeing, it also articulates a practical plan to actually implement the new ideas. Chapter 9 presents a comprehensive program of what has to be done, by whom, when, and in what manner. It includes checklists and timelines. Nearly everything it suggests is truly practical and/or being implemented already (at least in part, though incoherently) by current activists.

An Intellectual Synthesis

The program is an intellectual synthesis. It is a new paradigm having its own concepts and terminology but it is mostly an overlay upon existing elements of both theory and action. A whole lot of its components are already in place, even if not coherently and efficiently. It is a new way of thinking and acting about progressive action under a single *brand*, so to speak. Even though it is a complex paradigm conceptually as a synthesis of political philosophy, economics, behavioral theory, popular reform history, and modern technology, if people can understand the basic elements of balance, meaning and respect (BMR),and smart governance, they will understand the program.

The key to the program is to present a new social ethos with a single Voice and a single organization (i.e., the Brand) which has *focus and accessibility.* Focus and accessibility make it *easy* for people to understand and to participate.

Complexity

The program deals with some of the biggest issues of political philosophy and the biggest problems of contemporary society. Its vision and plan *can't* be truly simple! As a new theoretical paradigm it may be hard for some to understand and difficult for supporters to implement. (On the other hand, there is an elegance to the vision and the plan, meaning that all of the necessary components are in place, they fit well together, have an internal logic, and they tie well into current areas of social science and already existing progressive activities.) It is a long-term project, however. No one, of course, likes difficult, long-term prescriptions, like diets or breaking habits. We *could* offer an easier plan to understand and implement like many have but which *don't* work. Who wants that?

As an action manual the book works as a roadmap toward feasible progressive change. Importantly, there's no need to convince everyone in America of its value; as few as 15% of Americans can make this thing work. What's important is to obtain enough support to reach a tipping point where the number of supporters and the logic of the program make it become *the* way for Americans to think and live. The process is to organize a sequence of action events over an extended period of time and accept significant, but incremental results in the short term until the entire program becomes our new national social reality.

Will This Work?

No one has a magic wand and nothing attempting to fix America's biggest problems is going to be easy and happen quickly. Arguably, the vision is theoretically sound, the plan is practical, and we don't need to reach everyone (or even a majority) for this program to work. We can draw upon the overwhelming *desire* for change, existing resources, and the energies of a large existing activist population. The program starts out as a top-down program first offering its new concepts to intellectuals, high-profile cue givers, and progressive leaders. We start out with convincing influential types who can get the ball rolling by spreading the ideas to their followers and cue-takers. They will generate the other supporters that we need. For the most part, we need to just reorient existing attitudes of enough people and be persistent.

16

Importantly, we don't have to fight and defeat capitalism itself or the elite. The program is not anti-capitalism nor anti-wealth, but anti-*attitude* (individualism/capitalism.) Attitude change can make all the difference in the world. Think about where race relations were in the 1950's, gender relations in the 1960's, and sexual orientation ideas in the 1970's. Not much objective about the social world changed, only the mindsets.

Here is how this thing can work: We start with the relative ease of distribution of ideas. The structures will develop by top-down and bottom-up organizational movements involving high-profile influencers as well as grassroots ones. The open source digital development concept of lightly-organized collective contributions may act as a model of organizational development for the program. Importantly, this is no "Big Idea" movement requiring complex organizational or architectural elements, nor require a big-budget.

The program is positive and constructive, it builds up people to be the best they can be and governance to be the best that it can be. Supporters may be attracted to the freshness and originality of the new paradigm. Finally, the public values will eventually appeal to nearly everyone once they realize the feasibility of their implementation and the benefits to them both as individuals and citizens of what could become (again) the most advanced nation in the world.

Who May Support the Program (including some surprises)

Not every rich guy (or gal) is a self-interested, hard-core capitalist. We likely will have some members of the private citizen elite who share its values support it. Also, there will be many private citizens now who have been inhibited by their environment from acting upon their internal public values. They may be able to "flip" their mindsets and behaviors once the program has reached a comfortable tipping point. There may be marketers and public relations people who will be happy to serve public instead of commercial needs. Many ordinary Marys and Johns have been balancing private and public citizen interests all of their lives. They will be thrilled with the new humane environments in the workplace and consumer spheres. And, a lot of little people may obtain some self-respect about "evening the score," so to speak.

We Need the Elite to Support the Program

We *do* need at least some of the elite to buy into the program. We don't want to have to butt heads with the most powerful social group or have to try to overcome too much elite resistance. And, in any case, there are real benefits for them, too. As the elite is here to stay no matter what, we can make a win-win relationship where their financial and management resources can promote the advanced nation benefiting them as well as the little people. Some of the Big Ego-types can take on unique, positive leadership roles and become new American Heroes.

It Is Worth a Try

If you readers are interested in change there is no other significant plan. Our society is steadily declining. The little people, especially the weakened middle class, may start to get desperate. Something will have to give and it won't be pretty if the *elite* decides what it is. If the program works you will be helping yourself, your nation, and future generations. At a minimum, this program may be a noble adventure for some. It can be a meaningful personal and social experience more so than anything else–bigger then the civil rights movement and the 1960's counterculture, for example. For Americans, what is bigger than helping develop an advanced 21st-Century America with benefits for nearly everybody?

It may draw upon the pride of Americans who want to do the right things and to be the best they can be. The program ought to appeal to a new generation of youths who can frame their own futures. And, it may present for aging baby boomers one last chance to continue their positive influences upon their society in coordination with their children and grandchildren.

Summary–Chapter 2: The Characters

Public and Private Citizens

Forget about those old, tired, and mostly invalid social categories like conservative/liberal, Red/Blue state, Republican/Democratic, and the like. The most valid and most useful category for American political analysis is the private/public citizen one. Private citizens are individualistic, self interested, aggressive, competitive, and win-lose oriented. We can consider them as "Me" people.

Public citizens are dual attitude-oriented, partly towards self-interest, and partly towards community. They are "We" people. They try to strike a balance between their individual and community interests. They know that even the most solitary of personalities are still members of families, work groups, teams, communities, and the American nation. They are only moderately competitive (usually in low-consequences situations like sporting events) and favor win-win situations. In some cases, they will sacrifice their own personal interests for the good of the community, like soldiers do going into combat.

The private citizen/public citizen categorization articulated here represents abstract types. There are few who would be purely private or public citizens as nearly everyone exists somewhere on a continuum ranging from pure private interest to pure public interest. In any case, these categories are the most significant of all social categories and explain better than others the nature of decisions, behaviors, perspectives, and, especially outcomes in society.

Arguably, the "right-leaning" economic conservative component of the Tea Party has more in common with the "left-leaning" Occupy Wall Street group than they think! (Think of the populists on both the left and right in the 2016 presidential campaign.) They both are reacting to being screwed by a small group of self-interested (private citizens) in Big Business, government, or both.

Examples of Private Citizens

-Many Wall Street operatives in the 2008 financial crisis who aggressively profited on other people's woes or got the U.S. taxpayers to bail them out of their losses.

-Unions which insist upon maintaining jobs no longer relevant and benefits no longer appropriate which favor their members even at the expense of the economy, consumers, and the taxpayers (e.g., public sector unions.)

-Most special interests of all positions on every part of the political spectrum.

-Businesses and sports teams, for example which whipsaw communities into competing against one another and granting them more and more special benefits and subsidies at taxpayer expense for locating (or maintaining locations) in those communities. They make sure to keep profits private but expenses socialized.

-Manufacturers of worthless goods which they know they can market by deceptive means to unwitting consumers and the vanity goods industries which deliberately make insecure whole segments of the population (especially women) to convince them to buy their products so that they may "feel better about themselves."

Examples of public citizens

-Those people who reduce their environmental profiles by conserving energy, reducing waste, recycling, and the like sacrificing their own costs and time for the community as a whole.

-Charitable donors and those who subsidize disaster victims and the like.

-Soldiers and military personnel going into harms way on behalf of the nation.

-Contributors to online encyclopedias, review and recommendation sites; and those who post information, guidance of all kinds, and informational databases on the Internet, all on a volunteer basis.

-The ordinary Marys and Johns who work hard, raise good families, volunteer in their communities, handle themselves the best that they can with the resources they have, and never exploit anyone.

Private and public citizens generally have significantly different economic and other outcomes because of their attitudes. Because of the current individualist/capitalist environment we have in America, and the incentives favoring private citizens, public citizens generally get the short end of the stick. Often, they are just manipulated and exploited by private citizens. What kind of society accepts that "Good guys finish *last*?" (Only a society burdened by a perverse social ethos and obsolete governance and social relations systems. That has to be fixed.)

The private versus public category distinction *does not* necessarily equate to the haves and have-nots, conservatives versus liberals, Republicans and Democrats, the 1% versus the 99%, etc. The members of the private and public attitude categories span all of those groups. There are public citizens among the financial elite, too. It is the *attitude* that defines people, not their wealth, social positions, or affiliations.

The reality is that conventional social labels that we currently use are 18th-Century based. They are also artificially maintained (in large part) by interests which nefariously want to keep people (particularly the lower classes) divided and want to maintain permanent frictions among them. They want to keep them from developing a class consciousness recognizing that it is the elite class which dominates all the rest of us. Dividing the lower classes also inhibits *collective* leverage.

The trivial social categories like conservative/liberal, religion, ethnicity, etc. really don't even make much intellectual sense today. For example, both the Tea Party and the Occupy folks know that they are being exploited by members of both government and/or Big Business. They vary only in the details of exactly by whom and how it is happening and what to do about it. The differences among most religions, for another example, are quite trivial if you pay close attention to what each *essentially* provides–the psychological amelioration of the existential pain of personal responsibility and mortality and the value of organized community. They all even celebrate the same basic human events–birth, adulthood, marriage, and death. (There is no *good* reason for the prevailing frictions among religious groups. Either powerful habits or other, perhaps insidious, factors must be at play. E.g., ego and personal agendas of leadership.)

Intellectually, it is much more useful and feasible (and more valid) to organize people along the truly valid social category–either private or public citizen attitude--and get them to reorient their identities as members of a single group with common attributes–an American Team. That's what the program wants to do.

In addition, we don't want to imply that the private versus public attitude distinction is a "good guy" versus "bad guy" distinction. Philosophically, each can justify their attitude. After all, who can legitimately tell anyone that they should or should not have any concern about anyone other than themselves? In one sense, people are responsible for their own life decisions. We have to respect that existential decision, at the highest philosophical level.

Nevertheless, we still live, work, and exist together. For those who want to have a balanced society they will have to justify their position by relying upon proof of objective and subjective benefits, social morality influences, and other sorts of motivations.

Culture and Environment

The individualist/capitalist attitude which dominates American society implies a powerful set of "Rules of the Game." Those rules motivate individuals to be self-interested, competitive, aggressive, and short-term oriented. Citizens are framed by the rules to act in those ways whether they like it or not. Some do some don't. In some sense, it's not the people themselves responsible for many decisions and actions but the rules of the game. (That means significant social change has to come from a *new set of rules*.)

From a system point of view, the private/individualist attitude requires people to act only as workers or consumers; all the other roles one *could* take like family, community, team ones, etc. are really irrelevant and often are counterproductive to the economic system. (Mothers who balance their jobs and family, for example, typically get penalized in the workplace.). Not adhering to the system roles means getting regularly exploited, suffering negative career and employment consequences, and having high levels of stress, anxiety, guilt, and frustration. Private/public attitude balance is *not* a defining characteristic of Americans, in general.

Nonetheless, there are people and businesses which maintain a good balance between private and public interests. Some large set of businesses, for example, *are* public citizen-oriented while still making profits. They have to work very hard at it and have to accept perpetual competitive insecurities. Others keep a good balance while accepting the lumps which come with doing it. The object of those wanting balance is to make it *easy* for everyone to balance private and public interests.

Scientists have found evidence of what may be a biological basis accounting in part for private versus public citizen attitude. That means that people don't necessarily reason about what attitude is best for them. Current social science research shows that people are way less rational than believed in many ways and act mostly from deeply-rooted emotions, psychology, values, and especially habit. The truth is that most people don't think out their lives much in any detail–they just muddle through. That implies the significance of *social context* in determining attitude.

The Character of Nations and Society

The type of society one lives in may be the biggest determinant of attitude. If one lives in a community-oriented society, like say Canada or Scandinavia, individuals tend to have attitudes closer to public citizens. Those who live in aggressive, capitalist environments, like America and perhaps Russia, tend to have private citizen attitudes.

The profile of a private citizen-based nation is that it is typically innovative, creative, productive (and "creatively destructive"), individualistic, aggressive, warlike, insecure, has limited perspectives, has a large measure of economic inequality, is administrative and procedurally messy, has a low measure of regulation, and is coldly emotional.

For example look at the attitudes of the most defining party in America– Big Business--where the primary theme is "Business Is Business!" The implication of that attitude is a rejection of balance, ignoring of human meaning, and respecting little but economic success. It also is anti-collective and collectively irrational (as what is good for some aggressive rich guy is often bad for everyone else.) Why is *this* attitude so exalted by so many Americans especially when it is so deeply negative for the vast majority of them?-(see below.)

The typical profile of a public citizen-oriented society is security, organization, planning, coordination, multiple perspectives, a lower measure of political/economic inequalities, harmony, tolerance, peacefulness, and emotional warmth.

Good examples are the European Union which has modernized and rationalized a giant region covering two continents in terms of governance and social relations, as big a social advance as world history has ever seen. Another example of a public citizen environment maybe your childhood home. Your mom, for instance, didn't compete with you for resources or advantages; she didn't charge you (or put you on a tab) for your strained carrots, etc. She took care of you for reasons other than self-interest. She was a domestic socialist! It was the right thing for the family and she was a better person for it, too.

The Role of Intensity

Private citizens are more focused and intense; public citizens are less so. The focus and intensity of an individual or a small group is a powerful advantage against the diffused attention of a larger group. This is a well-known concept in organizational theory. Imagine a grand buffet table where private citizens aggressively scarf up everything they can take as quickly as they can while public citizens take only what they need and make sure others have fair opportunities to partake as well. The private citizens get most of the goodies (and *all* of them if they could.) The result is (depending on who's morality you apply) significant unfairness for most people.

The consequence of focus and intensity versus diffused attention is advantage and exploitation. The more it occurs and the longer it goes on in the economic and political areas the more income/wealth disparity there is. In time, we develop a dominant elite of private citizens.

For the most part, the ratio in society of private citizens to public citizens is low. Nevertheless, the influence of private citizens is way beyond what could be expected merely from their numbers. In America, certain groups are known for their focus and intensity–the financial elite, special interests of all kinds, political parties, and others. They dominate the economy, politics, policymaking, and even culture.

Attitude Makes a Big Difference

The attitudinal implications of individualism and competition are advantage and exploitation. Imagine, for example, an ordinary public citizen, Mary, interacting with a private citizen, Leonard, where they come upon a pie. They agree to split up the pie. Mary allows Leonard to slice the pie into two pieces which he slices into one large and one tiny piece. He then grabs the large piece for himself. If Mary was to slice she would have sliced the pie into two equal pieces and let Leonard have his choice of piece. Leonard considers Mary to be a fool; she considers him a selfish oaf. Nevertheless, he has the big piece of pie!

This mismatching of attitudes leads to economic winners and losers often based on unfairness and/or a rigged system. These kinds of transactions take place nearly every day in millions of situations. That helps explain why we have huge discrepancies in wealth despite roughly equal investments of time and effort between the classes.

Another type of private citizen exploitation, especially by Big Businesses, is when private citizens take for themselves things which really are public resources, like clean air and water, ocean minerals and fish, and use (deplete) them for their own profits. Businesses take advantage of public resources for themselves and leave pollution and other damages for the public and the taxpayers to clean up or to suffer from. This is known as the creation of operational externalities.This externality activity happens all the time to the detriment of the less focused, ordinary citizens, especially the taxpayers. From the elite viewpoint, they are either economic wimps, stupid, or choose not to want to play by the existing rules of the game. Too bad for them!

The private citizen propaganda machine (they own most of the communications media, influences most of the educational curriculum, and imposes their mores upon workers and others) has convinced most Americans that this situation is a *natural* state. It is a type of Social Darwinism fashioned into a whole ideology. What it really is is strategic elite class manipulation of the little people allowing the elite to dominate, (falsely) justify it, and get away with it. Sweet!

The General Makeup of the Public

A very rough guess is that private citizens naturally make up between 5 and 15% of the population, public citizens make up 25 to 40%, and an inert group called the "masses," makes up 45 to 70%.

That means that a small set of Americans dominate the rest of us, mostly out of will (and their Rules of the Game.). A lot of us don't like it and try to resist (e.g., reformers, activists, and complainers) without much success. And a large part, a plurality (or majority), are either indifferent, believe they are helpless, or just don't participate in social affairs for whatever reasons.

What the Dominance of Private Attitude Means for America

-an elite class
-a plutocracy
-economic injustice
-short-term perspectives in economics and politics
-environmental degradation/and other harmful externalities
-dysfunctional government
-almost perpetual group conflicts, often over trivial differences
-social pathologies like alienation, insecurities, and anxieties
-general public cynicism of most authority structures
-a breakdown of the social fabric

For those who don't like this state of affairs, there are four options:

1. Give up resistance and become private citizens themselves
2. Accept the fate of public citizenship with its disadvantages
3. Try in some fashion to convince private citizens to become balanced
4. Engage in serious pushback on the dominant elite class and its social ethos

None of these are truly good options as the first two are a form of surrender. The third has either been tried and failed or is just not feasible. The last one requires some amount of conflict, and most people don't like conflict.

For those willing to take some modest risks and assert themselves (at least for their self-respect) the pushback strategy articulated by this program may be the *only* realistic option. It implies conflict, but not as much as some may imagine (see below.)

What the Program Means to Everyone in America

The Classes:

1. The Elite

They're mostly private citizens. They will generally be in opposition to a pushback program. The effects for them would be less running roughshod over the little people in the economics sphere, less political influence, the ending of their incestuous ties to governmental officials, more regulation of business and self-interested activities to protect collective interests, an economic and political system reworked somewhat by the little people including a fairer allocation of the capital-labor value ratio, and for some, a loss of ego status.

All of this is really *not so bad* for the elite class. They will still go about their business but with a bit less impunity, earn a bit less, and not get their way in politics as much as they would like.

In addition:
-they will still keep most of their wealth, privileges, and status
-they will still have the legal government to protect their assets
-there'll be no beheadings or similar acts of retribution
-they will still be an elite!

Some of them may sincerely support the system. Current rich guys like Howard Schultz and Warren Buffett already show public citizen attitudes. Other fair-minded ones will recognize that the program's intentions are good. They will support less economic/political injustice and a smart governance American society. The enhanced emphasis on professional governance promises to solve major social problems which have resisted incompetent and/or insincere prior efforts, wasting government monies and credibiity.

There will be some more direct benefits for them as well:

-There will be unique leadership positions that some may be eager to fill, even for ego reasons
-Some may take pride in being part of a historical movement towards an advanced American society
-They will experience a more efficient government and economy, especially regarding *their* tax money
-They will see major social problems fixed for real instead of seeing their tax dollars thrown away at ill-conceived or futile projects
-They will benefit from the alternative meanings that will come from the humanity perspective of the program allowing them to address imbalances in their personal lives.

2. The Middle Class

There will be an exceptional opportunity to constrain or reverse their diminishing numbers and influence. Most will probably find appeal in:

-a more just allocation of income and wealth
-more political influence
-more economic security and fairness
-a new social ethos promoting life balance
-a new social ethos with public values more in tune with values they have now
-a new measure of respect and social status
-new opportunities to take ownership of local and regional social problems and issues through participation in the national and Local Councils

-reward and conditioning systems designed to make it *easier* for them to become better citizens and people
-a new identity and pride in themselves as American Team Members
-a recognition that there *is* a theoretical alternative to individualism and capitalism and it works

3. The Lower Class

These people are almost completely dominated by the elite. And, it's mostly not their fault. The imperatives of the current system almost mandate that they be losers. For advancement they will need a lot of help from government and informal institutions (especially the program's) as they are essentially without resources and leverage.

They will benefit in a variety of ways:

-they will obtain the same economic and other benefits as the middle class, as noted above
-they will have new pathways upward to middle-class and higher statuses
-they will be given new opportunities of employment, social status, and creativity
-they will be "brought up" as individuals by new opportunities, incentives, and conditioning programs and obtain the free time and resources to express their now latent creativity and social productivity

4. The Underclasses

These people include racial minorities, women, Native Americans, and smaller ethnic groups. There has been some progress by some of these groups (especially with feminism and racial integration) by their own efforts. However, for the most part, they still are second-class citizens. The program's theme of inclusivity may soften group identities and bring everyone into the Team Player group. They will have way more likelihood of achieving balance, meaning, and respect as *participants of the program* rather than as separate special interest groups, regardless of how determined they can be. They will have new leverage and status as part of the collective. They can become just *regular* Americans instead of hyphenated ones!

5. The Defenseless Class

These people include children, the disabled, the mentally ill, and many of the elderly. Many of them are strictly at the mercy of government and/or charity. They will have similar benefits as the underclass group, although they can't be expected to participate in the same ways as others. They will benefit from the collective perspective and rationality, more professional and rational governance and policymaking, and be welcomed into the new American Team.

Specific Personalities and Attitudes

1. Alpha Dogs

These people have big ids and egos which actually fit in well with individualism and capitalism. They like the liberty to will their way for whatever pleases them. No matter what the program does, they are not going away. They can feel constrained by the program (and be unhappy and perhaps obstacles) or, alternatively, recognize opportunities to become Big Actors in the movement in a positive way. These personalities may be channeled into positive outlets of leadership, innovation, and management of Big Projects. Those who can "play nice" with the rest of us will be a boost for the program with their resources, management skills, and personalities. Those who can't will have to be resisted and marginalized, but we prefer them to grab opportunities in a unique historical project where they can be National Heroes, of sorts.

2. Libertarians

For the most part, these people simply want to be left alone. They are big proponents of individual liberty, but theoretically and practically, there is a necessary balance between individual and group rights in any society. Fair-minded libertarians will accept that. People can argue over where the balances ought to be but for the most part balance is required.

Many may not like the collective themes of the program initially but the collective benefits include them no matter what, as they still are members of families, teams, communities, etc. On the other hand, seeing pushback by the little people on Big Business and special interest-dominated government should appeal to their political sensibilities. Libertarians also may appreciate the principled and rational decision-making principles of the program and its emphasis on reason and science. A lot of those constrained activities supported by libertarians, like over-regulation of relatively harmless recreational drugs and consensual activities of various kinds, will be liberated by more intelligent, rational governance processes.

In addition, the program is voluntary. No one has to contribute anything towards the public good although there is a pretty good history of libertarian-oriented people doing so. Think of the early Internet pioneers and the Open Source movement which has brought much of the greatest technology to everyone.

3. Fundamentalists

They are close-minded, intense, intolerant people who typically have extremely limited and odd focuses. They are unwilling to empathize, compromise, and are mostly irrational. They don't play nice with anyone else. They will need to be marginalized. The program has nothing special to offer them except for those benefits specific to economic/social statuses, as noted above.

4. Moaners and Groaners

Something in their psychological/emotional makeup make these people need to grouse and criticize as a matter of personality and habits. They probably make up 5 to 10% of the population but they're mostly harmless. Regardless of their attitude, they will benefit, too, in a lot of ways depending on their economic/social status.

5. The Masses

These people generally will remain socially and politically inert even though many of them will obtain huge economic and other benefits from the program. Some, hopefully, might be inspired by the activism and results of the program and become participants. Maybe the locked up latent creativity and productivity many of them possess will be released. They will benefit like the other lower classes noted, nevertheless, even if they simply do nothing for themselves or for the community.

6. Political Philosophies--Classical Conservatives versus Classical Liberals

The program spans many of the principles of both the conservatives and liberal positions. The difference between these two positions essentially comes down to who steers the "Ship of State?" The conservatives believe that they have the most at stake, more education and experience, better capabilities, and the confidence to handle the management of the nation.

The classical liberals believe that the conservatives are overstating the case of their value to society and are undervaluing the contributions of the lower and middle classes. Besides, the conservatives clearly steer only for themselves as they are too intensely self-interested. The lower classes don't want to take full control but only to have some significant influence. In addition, there is a respect aspect derived from the program for the little people which is important psychologically.

Conservatives should appreciate the program's intent of high personal and social aspiration and responsibility. The emphasis on values, both private and public, harmonizes with conservative ideals. The balancing concept ties into the conservatives concept of "a Good" life, that is, one not restricted to mere economic success. They should appreciate the emphasis on smart, professional governance.

Liberals should value the progressive social ethos, the set of public values, the respect for reason and facts, the active involvement of formal and informal governance in guiding behaviors, and the conditioning programs to bring *everybody* up regardless of social status.

7. Progressive Social and Political Groups

The emphasis on an improved social environment is key to lower-class improvement and reinvigoration of the middle class. Progressives and liberals should appreciate the balancing of elite and lower class attitudes, interests, and outcomes. Even though they may disagree with the overall paradigm and even parts of the plan, this movement could represent their only chance for success of a progressive agenda. Uniting under a single brand, focusing on BMR and smart governance and social relations, and being accessible to everyone is the key to obtaining the leverage needed for real pushback. History has shown that going it alone or in ad hoc coalitions with no coherent plan or organized leverage has failed consistently.

The Occupy Wall Street people should appreciate a *real plan* with a real chance of success, to go along with their wills, energy, and resources. That *combination* is what may make the difference between mere noisemaking and real change.

Socialists and Social Democrats, too, may find this to be the only chance for them to obtain any of their goals. They may support the new ethos and public values even though the program works *around* capitalism instead of trying to replace it or reform it. There is enough substance in the pushback concepts to effect real progressive results. They will appreciate the rationality and professionalism of the program and the informal institutions managed by the little people themselves even as the program rejects the traditional class conflict concept they have accepted for generations.

Some of the social outcomes may be similar to those of the European Union, Canada, and the Scandinavian countries where those societies appreciate a balance of private and public interests. What the European Union is trying to do represents a rough sort of model for an advanced America.

8. Economic Conservatives

The emphasis on personal as well as public character may appeal to them. They may appreciate the emphasis on *smart* governance, which is different than *small* government. They may have a greater appreciation for government jurisdiction and activity if there is a high level of trust in smart policymaking and operations as promised by the program. Fair-minded conservatives will appreciate the lessening of special-interest influences and the sandboxing of governmental officials from conflicts of interest.

Some of the more righteous or intense may relish participating in the shadow government taking on monitoring roles and influencing governance to comply with the new social ethos rules. While reluctant to accept more governmental involvement in people's lives, the social conditioning and public value incentives may appeal as they may produce the *results* that these people want, where their own strategies definitely will not.

9. The Tea Party and Social Conservatives

The Tea Party must be understood as having three types of people: a true limited government component, the evangelical component, and the "Trojan horse" component which really is made up of elite supporters who are insidiously aiding the elite and co-opting the intents of the authentic Tea Party conservatives.

The limited government component certainly would favor smarter and better (even if not smaller) government and a greater emphasis on personal and social responsibility throughout the society.

One problem is that the Tea Party has to be convinced that the government itself is not their real enemy. They need to know that the outcomes of governance which they object to most are not due to the idea of government itself but to the undue influences of special interests, especially the financial elite class as a whole. However, many blame the concept of government rather than the flaws and the distortions imposed upon it. For the most part, the authentic Tea Party people need to realize that government (as reformed in this program) is *their best friend*, as a protector against the elite and special interests which represent what they know as "crony capitalism." In effect, the elite so far has co-opted the Tea Party for it's own nefarious purposes and gotten them to unwittingly support more of the same unfair outcomes.

Why the mostly lower-class, working members of the Tea Party believe they have an affinity with the elite in restricting government is strange. Their strategy of stymieing governmental activity and in reducing budgets is actually counterproductive. It plays directly into the interests of the elite class which wants unfettered ability to assert their ids and egos. If these change-minded people want to obtain any beneficial social change it is going to be in a pushback of the elite class pursuant to a program like the one proposed here. Again, this type of comprehensive program may be their only chance of real success.

The evangelical component of the Tea Party really has no connection to the economics one even though it has made some odd social affiliation with the authentic economic Tea Party component. These people can obtain everything that religion is supposed to provide without engaging in irrational, inefficient, and unnecessary interference with governance and science. Religion has its place but not so much in the areas of science, education, and governance. The program deliberately wants to constrain their activity in public affairs to those uniquely valuable in their religion itself.

10. Geeks and Internet Gurus

These tech people are generally progressive and collectively-minded although many are libertarians. They, perhaps more than most, would value the program's emphasis on science, reason and facts. They ought to like the theme of smarter, more professional governance. Many of them are in actuality "digital socialists" who support public values, engage in community-minded projects like the Open Source movement, the open Internet, freeware and shareware development, and the like.

As a whole, these tech people have also pioneered a model of contemporary social organization in the Open Source movement which can guide the construction of the National Character Program itself. Also they have developed new types of pushback strategies like online boycotts and such which harmonize with the pushback functions of this program.

Some of these people would appreciate just the technological challenge alone of organizing a network of the little people and developing an accessible interface for them empowering them to participate effectively in pushback simply as a provocative technological challenge.

Summary–Chapter 3: The Setting

What in the Heck is Wrong in America?

You know your country is really messed up when even top members of the financial elite who have benefited more than anyone from the individualist/capitalist system plea to Congress to have their taxes raised! Some publicly acknowledge the system's excesses and support policy changes to even things out somewhat between them and the rest of us.

Our individualistic/capitalist American culture has more than merely class-based economic and political injustices but has fundamental *structural* elements which not only will maintain a permanent class hierarchy but inhibit the system from being suitable for governance in the 21st-Century. That is, it:

     1) Lacks a collective perspective

     2) Is not Smart and lacks a Brain

     3) Lacks medium to long-term time perspectives

     4) Is socially inefficient

     5) Lacks social character, and

     6) Has unfairness elements throughout.

     That's quite a list of flaws but they define, in most part, the setting in which we've lived since the 18th-Century.

What is Wrong in America?

The Structural Problems

1. It lacks a collective perspective in economics and politics
2. It is not Smart and lacks a brain
3. It lacks medium to long-term time perspectives
4. It is socially efficient
5. It lacks social charter
6. It has unfairness elements throughout

The Structural Problems

A. It lacks a collective perspective in economics and politics

The system can't even conceive of a collective perspective of *all* Americans with a collective rationality in governance and policymaking. The pervasive, "Every man for himself, win-lose," mentality directly leads to increasingly high public and private sector debt, dysfunctional government, irrational policymaking and wasteful budgeting, extreme partisanship (especially class-based whether recognized by the little people or not; the *elite*, on the other hand are well aware of it), incentives for corruption and crime, and widespread public distrust and cynicism.

2013 polls show that Congress, at least, is rated lower than cockroaches and colonoscopies. The rest of our authority institutions don't rate much better.

We haven't been a society of homogenized, small, independent farmers with little interaction with anyone else in a long, long time. Our contemporary society has become an incoherent layering of globalism; urbanization; and new demographics, technology, and social relations upon 18th-Century institutions and governance concepts. The old understructure has been unable to support a healthy society for some time now.

No wonder much of the rest of the world has lost respect for our governance systems. Even our Constitution document, once flaunted as the vanguard of sophisticated governance, is now considered by many theorists as archaic. America is respected for its military prowess and weightiness of its economy, but not much else.

Despite all of this obsolescence and decrepitude, there are no comprehensive, coherent ideas to address these issues. Not only is there a lack of vision of an advanced society but that absence generates increased divisiveness as people struggle to deal with the more pronounced frictions among private and public interests and defensive social attitudes. It seems as if either too many people believe those academics who have stated that our current system is, "As good as it gets," and that competitive and aggressive competition is required to survive, or that there are no compelling alternative theoretical narratives for significant change.

Our Governments Are *Too* Open and Accessible

The 18th-Century design of our governments emphasizes decentralization, localism and parochialism, diffused power, and limited jurisdictions. It also invites elected officials to become beholden to private citizens and special interests who have the focus, intensity, and resources to elect them and influence their legislative and executive behaviors. Those basic design principles have *some* value, of course, but our governmental processes are filled with officials locked into conflicts of interest and having no incentive to promote the common good.

How smart is it to allow officials to accept campaign contributions and other goodies throughout their tenures from special interests and expect honest policymaking and collective rationality? This openness and lack of professionalism nearly guarantees both policymaking and executive behavior will be captured by private and special interests for their own benefit.

There is a powerful but little publicly-discussed informal relationship called the "Iron Triangle" made up of the interaction of special interests, congressional committees, and departmental or bureaucratic officials. This relationship allows the manipulation of a distinct part of government or a policy by special interests. Much of our governance is operated by these Iron Triangles. What people think of as governmental "waste and inefficiency" is really the natural, necessary outcomes of special interests distorting governmental behavior. (That's why taxpayers pay $600 for a hammer, not because some official is just stupid.)

Even enforcement and auditing functions are captured by special interests. That means even the worst ripoffs of the taxpayers, even criminal behavior, persist because audits are absent or rigged and rules are riddled with deliberate loopholes while enforcement budgets are made insufficient. (The elite make the rules, don't forget.)

The lack of constraints on small groups' focus, intensity, and resources makes it easy for focused minorities to dominate even a much larger majority. As a whole, governmental officials are professional and competent (or can be) but are overwhelmed by the structure of our open and accessible institutions allowing private citizen behavior to defeat even the most dedicated public servants.

Furthermore, these 18th-Century principles prevent contemporary governments from addressing the far different and broader issues presented by American (and global) life requiring new ways of addressing both old and new problems and issues.

Elite Dominance Of the Economy and Politics

The individualist/capitalist ethos which dominates economics also has insinuated itself in much the same ways into our politics and governance. That has led to elite dominance in both spheres despite the chimera that "the people" control things by having the right to run for office and to vote for whomever they want. The little people control little of anything and the political processes don't provide for very much real democracy.

Not only is the elite dominance unfair but the lack of a collective perspective makes smart governance nearly impossible. There is a logic of individualism and competitive capitalism which leads to dysfunctional governance and irrational and unfair policymaking because the outcomes are meant only for the benefit of special interests and not for an "American" or the public interest, in general.

There are few reasons for the dominant elite class to support changing the status quo. Why should they? They have rigged the system for themselves and it has worked for them for centuries. What the little people need is a way to change much of this and especially eliminate the ability of the elite to regulate themselves.

For "smart" governance, we need a brain in governance and we have no chance of collective rationality and fairness without it. One big problem is that no one or institution in America is in position to promote any national (collective) interest. That includes the President (having limited powers) and Congress (captured by special interests), and Big Business (*the* biggest special interest.)

Not even political parties (even of the third party type) have incentives to work for the collective. In theory, the parties are supposed to broadly aggregate the interests of the entire public but really they aggregate supporters only for partisan *electoral* purposes. The rules of the game incentivize self-interest, even of large groups.

The two major parties are essentially the same in any case--elite-sponsored and protective of elite interests. If you have to point out a difference between the Republican party and the Democrat one, the Republicans are essentially merciless (in advocating elite interests) while the Democrats are not *completely* merciless. (They will spread some crumbs around for the little people.)

What some people call "oppositional" politics is not really the institutional checks and balances contemplated by the Founding Fathers but partisan competition between the two major (elite) parties. The parties act to oppose the incumbent one, not necessarily to check overreaching, but to gain electoral leverages. That includes resisting even positive policies for the nation. Some consider that attitude as a form of civil treason, but it is legal and apparently tolerated by most as, "Politics as usual."

No one or institution in the political sphere has the incentive or resources to consistently aggregate "American" interests and certainly not a true collective interest or rationality. We need *some* program, primarily run by the little people, to create a new American Team (which *will* have the collective perspective we need to rework what we have now.)

Who is Responsible for the Lack of a Common Good?

Some skeptics will say that there never has been or will be a common good as most people are naturally self-interested. Others might say that our 18th-Century constitutional system has drawn the right balances between private and public interest. In liberal democracy theory the "people" can adopt whatever institutions and policies they want as they have the voting numbers and a majority prevails. It is said that people in a liberal democracy get what they deserve and maybe we have. That would be sad and disappointing.

None of that theory suggesting that the little people are responsible for their own sorry status, however, is true, as explained above and throughout this book. Some would say that the system is *so* rigged that the little people have almost no good options and no chance of achieving any significant change.

However, we can, with the *right program*, rework society to recognize the significance of private versus public interest attitudes and to condition people to a new balanced social ethos, resulting ultimately in more favorable outcomes for the little people.

B. Our Governance Is Not Smart and Lacks a Brain

The individualist/capitalist ethos works against smart governance and the collective brain. Smart governance requires a collective perspective and rationality, public values, rationality and professionalism in decision-making and policymaking, respect for science and facts, multiple perspectives, and medium to long-term planning capabilities.

For the prevailing ideology, the rules of the private "market" supposedly make things work out without *any* sort of public thought of any kind, consideration of human values, or oversight by anyone, especially formal government. Individualism as an ideology presents a primitive jungle-like environment where an "invisible hand" is the prevailing guide for economic, political, and social affairs, in direct opposition to the brain concepts of the program.

An advanced 21st-Century society is quite a bit different. It goes way beyond jungle behavior and morality. It assesses the state of contemporary life and makes the necessary adjustments in governance and social relations to fit our current set of social facts and potential. We can't get to it now with what we have as we lack the high-level statesmanship that would be a *minimum* requirement to reform our system and even that would be insufficient given the overall overpowering constraints of the individualist ideology. An entirely new social ethos is necessary, together with the active involvement of new institutions of governance (e.g., the "shadow government" and the National Councils.)

C. We Lack Perspectives, Time And Frame Wise

Time Wise

As a rule, our institutions operate on short term perspectives and lack medium to long-term ones. A lot of economists have clearly identified the flaws of short-term perspectives in the business world. Some of those flaws have led to financial and economic crises which have affected nearly everyone, with the little people getting hurt the most. Without sufficient legal regulation (and enforcement) those crises will reoccur regularly. The elite class, however, generally does fine with this volatility.

The short-term perspectives in governance and social relations have not been articulated as well or publicly. Some include the near-ridiculous continual campaigning behavior of elected officials on short-term statuses, the deliberate avoidance of growing public budget deficits, the inattention to infrastructure deterioration and environmental degradation, and the ad-hoc policymaking processes ignoring the values of coherence, coordination, and deliberation, especially in war making decisions. Maybe, most important, there are no structures or processes to make the plans (and ideas) to deal with the looming permanently unemployed underclass of multimillions of Americans. (You won't even *find* many serious ideas about that in our current public discourse. Incumbent officials will let the *next* generation worry about that.)

There is no focused *constituency* for medium to long-term planning in governance. Even many families and small businesses do better than the government or Big Business when it comes to consideration of longer-term consequences. We need an institution and experts (like the Planning Council) with the credibility, resources, and support to provide the right perspectives and planning capabilities.

Frame Wise

Mostly everything in life can (and should) be viewed with multiple perspectives. Truth has multiple realities whether people want to accept it or not. Wise people (and governments) are empathetic to multiple views, recognize the ways all perspectives both highlight and conceal realities, and fashion decisions and attitudes based on this understanding. Lacking multiple perspective comprehension is a failure of empathy and creates "unshared perspectives" leading to misunderstandings, mistrust, confusion, frictions, and wars.

A philosophical analysis of the *capitalist* perspective reveals these "realities" (among others):

-The basic units of analysis are individuals and the transactions among them. Everyone is understood to be a rational actor trying to maximize self-interest. The most important goal of any interaction is the competing with someone else and winning. (Forget sincere considerations of family, community, team play, and altruism! If they are present it's because they operate *outside* of the system's logic.)

-The capitalist system has its own efficiency and rationality standards that do not correlate necessarily with human ones. For example, dumping milk or other products to maintain pricing level is rational for it even if hungry children would like to have that milk.

-Selling and marketing in themselves are more important than the nature and quality of products and services being promoted. Bombs, cigarettes, etc. are just as valuable as aspirin, medical care, and the like. The system focuses only on increasing supply and productivity and moving it in commerce, regardless of its human values for anybody.

-Real people are subordinate and irrelevant to the system itself which is much more important than the people who participate in it.

-The system has to engage in perpetual transactions regardless of the needs or wants of real people. Its own dynamics are *never* satisfied. Astonishingly, but true, if there ever comes a time when the needs and wants of everyone are *completely* satisfied (and they choose not to buy anything else) the economic system utterly collapses, with enormous negative consequences for nearly everyone.

Really think about concept over! That may be the most significantly absurd concept of all time, yet it remains largely unchallenged. *That* has to change! In essence, the system has its independent imperatives like the rogue computer, HAL, in the 1968 movie "2001: A Space Odyssey," which imposed its digital self upon the humans it was supposed to serve.

-The system is soulless, has no respect for human needs, and its internal logic requires perpetual transactions without any *ultimate* goal of any sort. It just continues. A more rational system *would* have an ultimate goal, like global happiness, or some variation of the "Good" life.

Capitalist principles present an overwhelmingly powerful ethos. Without the system having sufficient social character (as we are discussing here) there are a lot of negative consequences: It leads to personal objectification, anxiety, permanent insecurity, angst, and alienation.

Here are some typical (helpless) responses by real humans to this situation:

-obsessive consumerism
-escapism
-a grasping of hope for better in a future life (like heaven or wherever)
-personal meaning *substitutes* like celebrity worship and team sports affinities (Go Team!)
-the collecting of objects (thimbles, antique toys, artwork, etc.) for no utility reason, but only as a meaning *substitute*
-just mindless muddling through it all (e.g., "Going with the flow," as a type of avoidance strategy.)

The current structural incentives for actual human beings are for individual-oriented behaviors, purposeless lives (except for producing and buying for the system), and subordination to a soulless ideology. Probably most people, if they thought about it intellectually, would figure out that *This Is Not Right!* Why should the lives of nearly everyone be subordinate to an ideology that considers the needs and values of real people irrelevant, with the attendant consequences?

We can make a better world based on a theoretically-sound vision and a practical plan. It is time for people, especially public citizens and those with good social character, to start pushback.

D. It is Socially Inefficient

-The economy produces whatever it can convince people to buy rather than what is objectively useful and valuable. The defense industry, for example, has convinced the federal government to purchase hugely expensive hardware it doesn't need or even want. The crying need for better education for millions of youths, among other things, is largely ignored.

-There is a oversupply of luxury and vanity goods and a deficit of publicly-useful ones like well-maintained infrastructures, quality eldercare, and jobs and social positions for everyone. Why is a $30,000 handbag considered more valuable to someone than the same value dedicated to loans for small businesses, or even to deficit reduction? Why are these evaluations made primarily by the elite class rather than by some more rational, collective process?

-Planned obsolescence and waste of all kinds are often good (capitalist) economics.

-There is an absurd preoccupation with absolute economic growth regardless of utility and need (not even thinking of a more just allocation of capital/labor ratio.) More, more, more.... regardless of environmental sustainability, budget sustainability, etc. (Good thing we invented credit!)

-The primary incentives are for anti-collective and anti-human behavior and social disrespect for the vast majority of people.

-The latent potentiality of the little people to be as good, productive, and creative as they can be is suppressed by the imperatives to constrain them by the elite class solely to the roles of producing and buying. They have little time or resources to be anything other than worker bees, so to speak.

-Our economic/political processes result in spending over half the federal budget for war making purposes (mostly useless) and a tiny fraction of that spent on peacemaking and social harmony programs. How does that allocation become acceptable to a rational person or a *smart* society.

E. It Lacks Social Character

There is too much emphasis on making money and achieving status. Why is it that someone engaged in shady commercial activity which stops *just short* of crime still becomes a wealthy, blue-chip citizen? Many actions considered immoral but not illegal include shady tax avoidance schemes, pyramid schemes, and market deceptions of all kinds. Moving *closer* to criminal behavior–but not over the line–is more lucrative than acting *more* morally. (Why do we accept *that*?!)

-We should have a social status standard not of who is the best but one where *everybody* can be the best that they can be. The emphasis should be on empowering people to be as good as they can be (with social character) regardless of absolute level of achievement.

-We should have a social status standard allowing the producing of a population of *all* winners instead of just a tiny set of winners.

-Good guys should finish *first* instead of last. We are discouraging and penalizing pride in effort, volunteerism, public-service, patriotism, social harmony, and enhancement of the social fabric. That is a tremendous waste of potential!

-Too little effort is placed on bringing people together into harmony. Instead, we deliberately engage in divisive group identity conflicts for competitive, partisan, and/or defensive reasons.

-We need to reward the people who make themselves the best parents, spouses, citizens, workers, etc. instead of just those who make the most money. Millions of good parents, spouses, etc., are worth way more to society than mere dozens of even awesome sports stars or celebrities.

We Have a Lack of Proportionality

-We tolerate a market system which rewards celebrities and sports stars, among others, with vastly more income and attention than others arguably way more important to the society–doctors, teachers, first responders, and the like. We give multimillions of dollars for NBA stars and celebrities and considerably less to doctors and Nobel Prize winners. From a collective's point of view, this is perversely irrational.

-Not only that, those overpaid parties would do what they do anyway for a *fraction* of what they are getting paid. That reveals an irrationality in the market pricing system where stakeholders, like consumers, can be gouged by more focused business-types taking advantage of an unfairly structured business situation.

-We have distorted markets in many areas where not all stakeholders can participate in effective ways, like when sports team owners whipsaw communities to obtain tax subsidies and other goodies for private citizen benefit. Special interests can strong-arm municipalities to give millions to private citizens for sports programs when more significant social needs are shorted. Public opinion is typically deflected and/ or manipulated by the special interests.

Some people might propose regulatory schemes to try to adjust some of these market irrationalities but appropriate results can be had much easier and more effectively simply by creative use of the tax system, especially progressive tax rates. There may be no need to "interfere" in the pricing markets in any way, as a progressive tax concept can "capture" back the undue compensation relatively easily. This approach maximizes economic freedom while compensating the public interest for its exploitation.

Social Status

Science may support the idea that social status and ego matters may be hard-wired into social beings. Even so, our cultural mores overemphasize these things.

Individual achievements in many areas deserve acclaim, of course, but so do the small life achievements of the ordinary Marys and Johns. We need to honor and respect the good parents, citizens, workers, and the like, as they deserve. Millions of small life accomplishments add up to way more social value than that of the relatively fewer individual achievements.

We should honor and respect every occupation and support the least desirable ones with special compensation, at least for those doing those jobs honorably and well. Nursing home aides, garbage workers, etc., for example, ought to have reasonable compensation and benefits schemes to balance the harshness of their occupations.

The public citizen standard of *good social character* ought to be at least a complementary one to the one of net worth and social status. That involves recognition of the values of personal integrity, social character, and living a balanced life. Let us elevate the status of Great Soccer Moms, Great Teachers, and the like to more deserving levels.

Winning as Everything Is Too Much

-There is too much importance placed upon winning versus losing. Even a great athlete who finishes a micro-second behind an opponent in some competitions is often considered a loser. (Where is the perspective?)

-The excessive emphasis on winning, in whatever area, creates incentives to cheat. The prevalence of cheating is influencing our youths and others to accept that behavior as natural and acceptable. We want to turn that attitude upside down and incentivize the benefits of good social character.

-We have too-strong incentives to match artificial appearance standards using models with nearly impossible measures of perfection positioned against the 99.9% of the rest of us making nearly everyone feel insecure and inadequate. Marketers of vanity products and services make a lot of money *deliberately* making a lot of people *unhappy*. (Why do we tolerate this?!)

Capitalism has its place and its benefits for society but a complementary standard emphasizing a quality small life is just as important for a healthy society. When everyone has a chance to be a winner the likelihood of the Happiness Index rising is great. That may have a lot of positive spinoff consequences running throughout society.

Perhaps most importantly, we need to think what our life purpose is. We know what the existing system demands--more and more of the same purposeless consumerism, forever. At some point, individuals and collective society ought to think philosophically about the meaning of their social existence. We ought to set some ultimate goals for ourselves as human and social beings rather than allow the system to enforce its needs upon us. Think, for example, of global peace, broad economic justice, contentment, less stress and complexity, smelling the roses, and the like. Why aren't these the focus of social progress rather than GNP?

What Happened to Truth, Honor, Shame, and Trust?

-The excessive individualist/competitive ideology overwhelms traditional moral qualities that a healthy society needs to have. As "Good guys finish last" so do elements like truth, honor, trust, and integrity become diminished. They don't pay off. (Why *shouldn't* they pay off?!) Increasingly, we are allowing anti-social character traits to drive out good ones.

-The incentives to compete as self-interested individuals have compelled politicians, political parties, the news media, and many other parties to become aggressive partisans, even if they don't really want to. That has led much of public discourse to become "litigation language," (like lawyers in a courtroom) deliberately designed to evade truth and to advance private/special interests. Truth is unable to adequately compete against empty promises, lies, and bullsh*t designed to manipulate emotions of the public.

-A great deal, if not most, of public discourse on politics and economics is now filtered through invidious categories differentiating the public into (intellectually invalid) groups like Red versus Blue, Republican vs. Democrat, etc., for partisan and self-interested purposes. Where is the sincere, practical *American* category?

All of this has led to loss of faith by most of the public in valid standards of truth, honor, and trust. The capture of most of our authoritative institutions by special interest imperatives has lead to their loss of credibility and respect. Common survey results indicate extremely low levels of respect for nearly all of our social institutions like our own governments, Big Business, political parties, marketers, and more, all of which are perceived as untrustworthy.

-In addition, the traditional role of leadership has turned upside down as our so-called leaders pander to constituents instead of *educating* and *guiding* them in the responsible fashion formerly expected. The attentive public is justified in being distrustful, cynical, and frustrated by the institutions and leaders who used to be credible authorities. (Who *can* we trust?)

-The traditional social standards of personal responsibility have eroded so much that even the most egregious liars, cheaters, and exploitive individuals can not only benefit blithely from their behaviors but rehabilitate themselves fairly easily, often aided by capable public relations teams and compliant news and social media sources. The public is either too easily fooled or too easily forgiving. In any case, that attitude has to be changed. We need to hold these people more accountable. Personal responsibility has to be restored, and it will take a new set of public values (perhaps as proposed in this book.)

Furthermore, we have had a great dumbing down of intellectual and aesthetic standards. The inability of the vast majority of people to avail of higher education because of structural constraints has contributed to that decline, of course. However, there are seemingly deliberate efforts by popular arts producers to condition the public to disrespect education, work ethic, manners, and personal responsibility. (Anyone who pays attention to Hollywood moviemaking knows what we are talking about.)

There obviously is a market for this entertainment but that doesn't mean that there isn't one for cleverly produced materials which support *positive* social character. Movies and television shows of the 1950's, for example, while still wildly entertaining, also contained lessons and positive role models. This alternative approach would act to bring people *up* and to reinforce positive social character.

If we create a new social ethos emphasizing truth, honor, trustworthiness, and the importance of shame (i.e., penalizing shameful behavior) we will have better people and citizens, a better democracy, worthwhile social progress, and become an advanced nation that nearly everyone can admire.

F. It Lacks Fairness

Economic inequality in itself is not necessarily a bad thing but an extreme level of it is. At a minimum, it shows social disrespect by the elite to nearly all other Americans. More importantly, it has created a situation where the lower classes have suffered enormous harms some of which may continue to persist for generations, in regards to housing, healthcare, long-term income needs, domestic stabilities, higher educations, and more.

There has been a significant collapse of the social safety net since the 1980's. The elite has eliminated American jobs and benefits; they've switched risks of pensions to workers; they've switched risks of healthcare to consumers; CEO's outrageously exploit compensation schemes; the scientific enterprise is becoming owned by Big Business thereby losing its credibility; we have a plutocracy in governance; many school curriculums are run for and by Big Business, formerly authentic news and journalism sources have become mere entertainment media or propaganda machines; and even wartime battlefield decisions are being made by *military hardware representatives*. (Whose interests are *they* serving?)

We have had a significant decline of the middle class since the 1980's in both economic affairs and political influence. The great unions which supported the middle class and other progressive issues are no longer very great.

The lower classes are in the position they are now not because they have given less effort, become less productive, become deficient in capabilities or motivations, or even lost out in a *fair* competition with more capable competitors. The huge disparity between the outcomes of the classes has not been because of objective factors but because the elite realized that they could dominate and *could get away with it*. (They have rigged the system, remember.)

They have. And, beyond all of that, they have an "in-your-face" disrespect for the little people tending towards disdain.

Furthermore, American capitalism and it's aggressive attitude has expanded to the entire world, where we are not only attempting to dominate foreign competitors but to undermine the decisions and activities that other societies have made towards progress in more advanced governance. Take the European Union, for example, where the historical capital/labor balances are now being adjusted significantly in favor of capital primarily because of the imperatives of global capitalism, American-style.

Just taking a historical view of the status of the little people, how can working harder and better, sacrificing more, accepting more risk and insecurity, maintaining civil standards of behavior, and trying to improve their conditions peacefully and ending up in a *worse* position be considered *Fair?* Not when the elite is living in a New Golden Age by aggressively playing a rigged system. (It's the Rules of the Game, again!) Let's have New Rules!

Summary–Chapter 4: The Back Story

1000 to zero!

That's roughly the ratio of (post-Great Recession) calls from all kinds of prominent people for significant change of our economic-political system to new, practical programs to make those changes happen. That's too bad, but when we have an increasingly dysfunctional society for most of us and a very long history of disappointments, it's understandable that new ideas are rare.

Some people are still proposing tweaks to the system like simplifying voter registration rules, increasing the minimum wage, repealing the Supreme Court's "Citizens United" decision which cut down most limits on campaign contributions, and other rather wimpy and ultimately futile ideas. For example, the agenda of the hyper-active Tea Party, essentially, is to stonewall policymaking and to tear down the government to spite parties unlike themselves who may or may not be really responsible for their frustrations. They seem not to have thought out clearly the consequences to other citizens, to the United States's financial credibility, and even to *themselves* of this willfully destructive approach, as weakening the government further will leave the elite class to *completely* dominate.

Most people wanting significant change don't know if *anything* can be done.

Historical Perspectives

The elite has always dominated American society and, up to recent times, there may not have been anything *anyone* could do about it. For most of that time:

-the productive capabilities of the nation were sufficient to maintain only a minimum physical existence for most people

-the lower classes lacked sufficient information and knowledge about economic and political affairs

-they had little ability in the political arena to leverage to assert their numerical superiority against the elite despite the formal existence of democratic institutions providing for majority rule

-they had no class consciousness, solidarity, or organization

-they lacked a sound vision of what could be and how to get it even if a suitable vision *was* available

-there were pathways for a good number of the most assertive and ambitious of them to move up in class status especially in the period when the great labor unions had influence, thereby easing the pressures for social change from below.

20th-Century Advances

There have been great advances in nearly every aspect of American life *except* for governance and social relations. Nearly every "object" area like technology, medicine, transportation, communication and others have made major advances to increase productivity, manage both assets and people, and to even prolong human life (but not necessarily increase the *quality* of it.).

Looking back at the last century, at least, some would point to these handful of American and global events as significant *social* achievements in the areas of class fairness, smarter governance, and better social relations:

-The development of the American middle class in the mid-20th century

-the implementation of a significant social safety net with the Great Society programs of the 1960's and 70's

-the creation of the United Nations

-the creation of the European Union, with its themes of smart governance, rationalization, inclusion, and diminution of frictions due to trivial social differences (like nationality, ethnicity, etc.)

-the development of coordinated worldwide financial, monetary, and trade rules and multi-national organizations

-the reduction of *legally*-based discriminations in many parts of the world relating to race, gender, the disabled, (and in the early 21st-Century) same-sex unions

-and, to some extent, a diminution of tribalism due primarily to the educational effects of increasing interactions of all types among multiple nations and ethnic cultures

However, the *theoretical* possibilities of social change have paled compared to the current realities. We are still burdened with much of the same issues we've had for centuries– wars and social group conflicts, widespread economic injustice, discriminations of all kinds, poverty, and other social ills. We have really underachieved as human beings in terms of governance and social relations.

For Americans since the 1980's at least, things have actually gotten worse for the country overall as our governance systems have become increasingly dysfunctional and social frictions have increased substantially. Worse, things have *really* declined for the little people:

-the capital/labor value allocation has shifted significantly more in favor of the elite

-the lower classes have stagnated or lower incomes, despite greater productivity

-only a small minority of workers maintain pensions, decent health care programs, and other similar employment-based benefits. Healthcare risks and post-employment income risks have shifted from employers to employees and even the status of "employee" has evolved for many into "independent contractor" shifting risks and costs to workers

-the organized labor movement has been nearly crushed, diminishing the only effective pushback element to date to elite dominance

-globalism has allowed the elite to export capital and employment opportunities to other areas of the globe effectively using the logic of "capitalist efficiency" to lower standards *everywhere* in compensation schemes, environmental protection, etc.

-the social safety net that supports millions of Americans and strengthens the social fabric has been significantly reduced.

Some may characterize all of this as a reneging by the elite of the social contract which existed for some generations between them and the lower classes, undermining the balance between their interests and those of the little people. They have learned that they can get away with it, and they have.

Why Can Anyone Expect Change Now?

There have been some objective changes in America in recent years realistically supporting new opportunities for significant social change:

-the productive capabilities of the economy have made overall improvement in the physical lives of most people presenting a lot of them with disposable time to devote attention to political matters

-many more people, especially in the middle-class, are more educated, wiser about economic and political matters, and savvy with new technology

-the Internet has made access to databases and information sources about economics and politics never before available, accessible to nearly all

-new technological tools like social media means and an advanced understanding of the power of communications have given the little people way more opportunities to become informed, engaged, motivated, and mobilized. As proposed here, a network of the little people (the Local Council) utilizing an easy-to-use computer interface can provide leverage means to the lower classes never available before

-experience of relatively recent successful social change movements, including civil rights, feminism, and others, have provided models of thinking and acting which may apply to efforts for *economic and political* change (provided there is a theoretically-sound vision and practical plan.)

-we live in a time where the power of ideas and values can be more readily engaged in a social movement by new technology and influence methods.

In other words, the lower classes can leverage their numbers and consumer power as never before. The resources are there and the will seems to be there. All of these things add up to Big Time "disruptive" possibilities of economic and political affairs.

The Power of Reframing

New ways of seeing and thinking, framed as conceptual "paradigms," can effectively alter society in big ways. Think of the civil rights and feminist movements as major examples. Think, too, of how right-minded, fair-minded people giving attention to the issue of tobacco smoking (which was an "invisible" issue for generations) have "flipped" society's attitude *against* smoking, with all of its attendant legal, social, and practical implications. (Let's not forget the historical examples of subjective framing power ending the feudal system in the 15th-Century or the termination of the monarchies in the 19th-Century.)

If we can get society to think of blacks, gays, and other minorities as "regular" people, females as equal citizens, and have flipped smokers to accommodate to non-smokers instead of the other way around we have a decent chance to train Americans to view people as private or public citizens and insist upon the private ones accommodating to the rest of us. After all, it is not only fair, but *smart,* in terms of governance and social relations.

In some cases, objective realities are not even significantly implicated in major social movements as it was the new subjective ways of seeing and thinking that were sufficient to alter social realities. When it comes to the individualist/capitalist ideology, our new paradigm doesn't intend to destroy it, replace it, or reform it much but posits a *complementary* ideology alongside of it. That means instead of mere smokers "going outside," private citizens, in a sense, will be going outside. It will be a change of attitude which will eventually imply significant objective changes in social realities.

The Possibility of Political Economic Change

The paradigm shift of new ways of seeing and thinking we are proposing is a framing technique. It is essentially a subjective change of mindset.

Philosophically, we live in a world of object where physical laws control us yet we also control that world by subjective ideas, attitudes, and values. There is an inherent tension between object and subject and what becomes our realities often depends on what we *will it to be.*

We are not going to change the laws of gravity nor the laws of economic "scarcity," but we can change our way of dealing with each other from being predominantly individualistic and competitive to that of being collectively-minded and tolerant of trivial differences. Mindset *can* create new realities. To make that work we have to believe that it will work and try it.

-In the 1950's who would have imagined we could elect a black man as President of the United States?

-In the 1960's who would have imagined a female CEO of a major corporation or an entertainer flaunting her sexuality on primetime television?

-In the 1970's who would have imagined the mayor of New York City presiding over a gay marriage?

-In the 1980's who would've imagined a global communication network accessible by nearly everyone set up and run, in large part, by volunteers and at little or no cost to users?

Public citizens and the lower class *can* end the domination of private citizens and special interests over the rest of us, obtain BMR, and implement smart government principles. Those things may be as obtainable as was a black president sixty years after the Jim Crow era.

What Will *Not* Work

1. Elections. The electoral system is rigged in favor of the elite and its capitalist ethos and no personality of whatever quality can overcome the imperatives of the system. Forget electing the new Political Hero. (As they say, been there done that.)

2. Changing party administrations. There is no significant difference between the two major parties as both are captured by the elite. Throwing out one party in favor of the next is simply an example of rotating elite groups. (Been there, done that.)

3. Third parties. The imperatives of the present system make third parties impotent even if they overcome enormous structural obstacles to get elected. In any case, they will still be subject to participating *inside* the system which allows dominance by the elite.

4. Legal reforms even of major proportion. It is the individualist/capitalist *ethos* which controls laws, politics, and governance. The rules, institutions, and processes merely derive from them. Without changing that ethos there'll be no significant change at all. The elite, in essence, will continue to regulate themselves. (Been there, done that.)

5. Revolution. First, there is no distinct target, as the problem is in the individualist/capitalist ideology, not necessarily specific personnel or institutions. Secondly, there is no alternative which can completely replace capitalism. We wouldn't want to even if we could because capitalism really does have many virtues (the pricing system, low management demands, etc.) Thirdly, as shown by the Arab Spring regime-change failures, there has to be a comprehensive plan of what is to replace any system and a practical way to implement it.

All of these options are theoretically flawed, incomplete, or not comprehensive enough to ensure significant change. We need something new and better.

The Back Story -What Won't Work

1. Elections

2. Changing Party Administrations

3. Third Parties

4. Legal Reforms even Major Ones

5. Revolution

"Been there, tried that"—no help and no change.

Summary–Chapter 5: The Functions

After ruling out elections, changing parties, forming third parties, legal reforms, and revolution, what else is left? We need a sound new vision of what a 21st-Century American society can and should look like.

A New Social Paradigm

It ought to be pretty clear that our 18th-Century ideas and institutions are obsolete and need updating and/ or replacing in some significant ways. The economic injustice issue is just obvious and must be addressed and the persistent and worsening fighting among ourselves (especially little people against little people) seems primitive and irrational (as well as counterproductive.)

What seems common among nearly everyone is that they feel their society to be unbalanced between the aggressive private citizens who acquire most of society's goodies and the rest of us, that there is a disconnect between the economic system's needs and human values. And, that most people get little, or no respect, even when doing right by their employers, families, and communities. Furthermore, many people question why an educated, supposedly civilized population contains so many (mostly irrational) social frictions, together with an extremely dysfunctional governance system.

Sound theory tells us that replacing capitalism is not an option but that a new social movement adding an additional, *complementary* social ethos to our basic liberal democracy demanding BMR and smart governance and social relations does makes good sense and is feasible.

These are the functions of a new social movement and of the National Character Program:

The Functions

-a new social (public citizen) ethos

-a brain in governance

-a shadow government

-a citizens' pushback network

-public citizen conditioning programs

-rewards for public citizen behaviors

-membership in Team America

-development of a new set of leaders, managers, and bridgers, utilizing in part a specialized academic curriculum made a part of a new National University.

A. A New Social Ethos

A new social (public citizen) ethos will contain:

-a set of new public citizen values

The Functions of the Movement

1. A new social (public citizen) ethos

2. A brain in governance

3. A shadow government

4. A citizen pushback network

5. Public citizen conditioning programs

6. Rewards for public citizen behavior

7. Membership in Team America

8. A new set of leaders, managers, and bridgers developed by a National University

-enhanced attention to the meaningfulness of the distinction between private and public citizen attitudes. Ideally, citizens will balance private and public attitudes. Those who do will be rewarded. Those who don't will be pressured to accommodate to public citizens, a reversal of what we've had for generations.

Those dual attitudinal frames will be in a permanent tension requiring constant adjustment by individuals and program institutions and management. Making that attention almost automatic will be important. (That's where a new social habit fits in.) No one wants more tension in their lives, but there always has been tension in America between the private and public citizen attitude which has been rarely articulated and which has been cloaked in public consciousness and discourse by the elite which wants to divert attention away from their selfish actions and exalted status. They don't want people to know how rigged the system really is in their favor.

-smarter governance and social relations

-respect for the small life and good social character

-inclusivity and the formation of a collective perspective represented in a new social category of Team America members.

B. New Public Values

Here is a list of public values:

-a balancing of private and public citizen attitudes

-a collective prospective and collective fairness

-trustworthiness in government, Big Business, and public society

-economic efficiency and meaning from a collective perspective

-enhanced respect for science and reason in social problem-solving

-pride in oneself regardless of status

-consideration of multi-perspectives

-humility based on the limitations of knowledge and social management

-tolerance of trivial social group differences.

All of these add up to balance, meaning, and respect (BMR), together with smart governance and social relations.

From one perspective, we are facilitating a more *female* orientation towards society emphasizing a better balancing of the aggressive, competitive male nature and the more community-oriented and nurturing female nature. Too much of the masculine nature leads to a solitary, unhappy, and unfulfilled life. Too much of the female means potentially dangerous economic and practical risks. We can learn how to balance these attitudes in social life, especially given the plentiful resources we have now.

C. The Shadow Government

We have had centuries of experience with elite-dominated governance and politics. While regulating us they also regulate themselves. We know how *that* works!

We can't trust the elite nor our government as presently structured. Besides a whole lot of systematic reforms of existing government, like sandboxing officials to eliminate undue influence and conflicts of interest (as detailed in Chapter 7), we will keep a sharp eye on who is doing what in governance and audit what happens so the public knows what is going on and who is benefiting, if not the collective. Our own informal institutions, especially the Local Council, will constantly monitor government activities in most areas. We will make public disclosures of undue private citizen activity, corruption, and/or incompetence; mobilizing reactions of public citizens (and the little people) to those things; and reporting those bad acts to our enforcement institutions to suggest Action Plans (i.e., pushback) to counter them.

In order to achieve what we need *requires* forceful pushback upon the individualist/capitalist ideology and its institutions. The Action Plans will make up a big part of the pushback function of the Program. They will include shaming strategies, boycotts, and other similar leveraging of lower-class numbers and consumer weight.

The monitoring, disclosing, and pushback functions will operate on national, state, and local levels. This kind of attention will be directed towards both government and Big Business, together with a lesser focus on society in general. We will insist in all aspects of government on a collective perspective, rationality, competence, and trustworthiness and respond appropriately if they are absent.

Beyond monitoring what is happening in government, the shadow government will also contain a handful of other informal institutions, especially the Planning and Problem-Solving Councils. They will be part of the brain in governance (see below) and add functions and capabilities no other large-scale institutions in American now have--collective perspective and rationality, longer-term planning, problem-solving for national problems, professionalism, and credibility.
.

D. A Brain for Society

We need to add to our governance a brain having a collective perspective and rationality and planning and problem-solving capabilities. We can't have quality policymaking and decision-making without being smart.

 Not being *smart in governance and social relations* in the 21st-Century is akin to:

-not recognizing the values of *science* in the 17th-Century

-not accepting the moral force of *democracy* in the 18th-Century

-not understanding quantum mechanics and relativity in the 19th-Century and the meaning that *multiple perspectives and points of view* have for understanding both natural and social affairs, and especially human relations

-not accepting race and gender *equality* in the 20th-Century

We may be at a new historical era now where fair-minded people recognize that we *can* achieve smart governance and social relations if we approach change in the right ways emphasizing public values and collective fairness, together with the enforcement against the dominant ideology by pushback strategies.

The brain in society refers primarily to the operations of the Planning and Problem-Solving Councils but also to the generalized rationality and professionalism which should permeate governance at all levels based on the examples set by the National Councils. Those governments will be guided with the templates of action and decision-making created by the program.

Here are some *substantive* issues which these Councils will address:

-effective regulation of the financial sector to remedy the risks and injustices to the little people

-adjusting the capital/labor value allocation ratio to be fairer for the little people

-reworking of the tax system for both fairness and social utility

-peacemaking, including minimizing trivial social group differences domestically, but also establishing templates for positive social relations between our nation and others in the global arena

-rationalizing governments for cost efficiencies and accessibility

-And many more.

Smart governance will earn credibility and legitimacy with the public because of its collective perspective and fairness, rationality, competence, trustworthiness, and professionalism.

Compare this smart approach to what we have now, the invisible (i.e., incoherent) hand in economics and its correlate--messy elite-dominated faux democracy in politics. Those approaches have no ultimate goals, little consideration for planning, and no standards of achievement or measurement except for growth in the quantity of the economy and low levels of taxation whether those things make sense under particular historical circumstances or not. (Maintenance of elite dominance is the primary goal, of course.)

Think of how the governance system has responded to the (trivial) proposal (2010 or so) to increase efficiency standards among incandescent light manufacturers and how it decides when and where to go to war--irrational resistance in the former and partisan politics in the latter. We continue policies which nearly every fair-minded, intelligent observer knows are wrong (e.g., the war on drugs, incoherent healthcare delivery systems, etc.) but don't change.

Some might say, that we're making fools of ourselves over and over. What kind of system is that? Where are the considerations of human values, happiness, security, collective efficiency, true problem-solving, and fairness?

We have persistent social problems which have never been fixed and not even addressed with appropriate problem-solving approaches. Because the *process* is bad, actual problems can't get fixed. And, the elite (which pretty much runs the show, so to speak) has nearly no interest in really fixing them because they are rarely negatively effected by those problems or can evade them and don't care much about anyone else.

There have been *some* intelligent attempts to bring new approaches to governance, like the military base closing commissions, and the 2010 Simpson/Bowles commission to address governmental deficits. While achieving some modest successes, those projects were limited, ad hoc, and still not immune from the basic flaws in the system which prevent smart governance. That's not nearly the best we can do.

In order to obtain *smart* governance, we need the following:

-A collective perspective and rationality

-a new set of institutions run by the little people to oversee traditional legal government (e.g., the shadow government and the Local Council)

-systemic reforms in existing government to minimize private citizen/special interest influence upon governmental officials and policies

-new professional institutions to add capabilities to our governance systems not present now (e.g., the National Councils)

-greater emphasis on scientific and technological approaches to problem-solving.

E. The Citizen Pushback Network

We need a *single, accessible* public citizen pushback network for a number of reasons: 1) Only the little people themselves will be motivated to fix their own problems. They can't rely any longer upon the elite; 2) The lower classes can leverage for once their voting numbers and consumer weight; 3) Oversight of the American economy and political system is such a big project that it has to be done by a widespread, grassroots-based, informal structure of citizen volunteers; and 4) we can make it relatively *easy* for the ordinary Marys and Johns to participate.

Pushback of this sort may be the only approach to balancing the existing system that can be effective. (Remember the individualist/capitalist system is not going away.)

Some methods of pushback would include:

-disclosures and declarations of opposition to bad acts by the elite and Big Business in governance and economics

-public shaming strategies

-consumer, labor, etc. protests, etc.

-boycotts of various sorts of institutions, industries, and products

-civil resistance and other techniques (modeled after the civil rights and feminist movements)

-strikes and other similar workplace strategies

-traditional means like voting, lobbying, etc.

How to Set up the Network

The pushback network will rely on the individual participants having their own computers and/or mobile devices. Those devices will be complemented by data and other servers and Internet-based tools. Our tech specialists will create a network linking all of these people and components together. There are two keys to effectiveness beyond the hardware infrastructure—an *easy-to-use* accessible user interface and the formation of a *habit* by participants of accessing the Local Council network on a regular basis, like they check the weather, sports scores, and the like now.

The user interface will have sections about Council news, surveys and polls, pending Action Plans, etc. with prompts to get people to give attention and participation even for just a few minutes a day. We don't need much more than that, for the most part.

There will be a central command center for collecting and distributing information, aggregating responses from surveys, etc., and in formulating and enabling Action Plans. Members of the Support Council, especially, will be active in developing the habit of attention to the network by the public.

We want the user interface experience to be a conditioning tool to both promote progressive behavior and empower the little people to engage in effective pushback. A model of how an Action Plan may work would be the SOPA events of 2013 where online activists mobilized responses from Internet users and turned back efforts by special interests to unfairly regulate the Internet for their own purposes.

The Local Council

The Local Council will be the backbone of the program representing the large majority of program supporters and providing the numbers and consumer power to give leverage to its operations. It will be a counterweight to the elite and the existing social ethos and will be the biggest and most important element of the pushback functions. It will monitor, disclose, and act in opposition to governmental and Big Business bad acts. The Council will also represent a new social group, the American Team, promoting a new sense of inclusivity including all Americans as a collective.

As a coherent, accessible communications network it will facilitate the ease-of-use that is essential to the participation of the number of people we need to be effective.

Public Citizen Conditioning

For the most part, the social environment influences citizen attitude. Where the structural incentives are for individualism, as in America, citizens will tend to act as private citizens (even if only in a defensive position.) However, if we install an ethos of private/public balance, many people will respond to public citizen values especially if their friends, neighbors, and other social influences support them, too.

We can condition a public citizen attitude with incentives (see below), the influence of high-profile cue givers and role models, forming a hospitable environment supporting public citizenship activities as a habit, promoting templates of "good" behaviors, and by demonstrating objective benefits and achievements. Those benefits will include social-level problem-solving, greater security, happiness, relaxation, respect, and more.

The private citizen incentives are powerful and persistent, however, so *continuous*, effective social conditioning making the private/public balance the "right" choice will be necessary.

We also have to understand the limitations of personal choice and responsibility. While a lot of people believe that citizen behavior is the outcome of cognitive decisions, social science shows that this is a myth. Scientists have proven that most people act on the basis of habits, emotion and psychologies, and deeply-seated values. We are not going to influence a majority of citizens by appeals to reason. We need sophisticated strategies of many types to get people to act as public citizens.

We influence behavior primarily by conditioning—creating new, better habits. That conditioning includes a conducive environment and having accessible templates to guide everyday behavior. These templates will provide guidance on how to "do things right" and make it *easy* for good citizenship, good parenting, good electoral practices, and the like.

Not only do we need quality templates we need *permanent* conditioning. There's no reason to think that once someone has reached adulthood that they are then fully responsible for their attitudes and behavior. Think about the most significant conditioning agents in society now, Big Business and marketers. They are relentless and persistent in conditioning people to do what they want. (i.e., buying from early childhood to the end of their days.)

The little people, especially, will benefit from continuing help. We have to make it *easy* for everybody to be good and to do good. Although some people may call this a "nanny state" approach, this is no different than what nearly all cultures and social groups have done forever. We can't rely on the idea of personal responsibility to be very relevant; we must make public citizen behavior a *habit* consistent with people's deeply-seated values.

Here are some means to accomplish that:

-clear articulation of the public citizen attitude and goals so everyone understands the basic ideas of what they ought to be doing

-cue-givers and role models

-media influences

-school, workplace, and cultural curricula

-templates of all sorts relating to everyday behaviors

-nudging behaviors imposing "default" decisions that work best for people while allowing them to opt out if they choose

-a reward system for public citizen activities.

An example of how this conditioning may work is with public smoking policies. We have only in recent decades made "visible" the public effects of smoking. Although people can decide to smoke or not for themselves, the externalities are deleterious health outcomes for non-smokers, enormous medically-related costs to taxpayers, and enormous social costs to families and communities.

Interested people have articulated the reasons for an anti-smoking attitude and corresponding policymaking. We have engaged various strategies to discourage, prevent, and condition people not to smoke. And, most importantly, we have *flipped the social attitude*—that smokers have to accommodate to non-smokers, rather than the other way around. Our movement intends to flip the private attitude to that of a public citizen one, in a similar way.

Here are some public policy areas that may benefit from this type of social conditioning: individual and family health behaviors, continual education, projects to ameliorate irrational trivial differences among social groups, good citizenship, and stewardship of the environment.

F. A Reward System

This is a form of conditioning but it is more. In part, it is a matter of fairness for those public citizens who sacrifice for the good of the collective. It also promotes the ideas of good public citizenship and quality social character.

G. Bringing Everyone into the Movement

Ideally, the movement will obtain a rough consensus of Americans for the worth and importance of the new social ethos. There will be ideological opponents, of course, and the largely inert–the masses. Nevertheless, the program's essence is the sense of the collective–that means all of us, including the elite. There have to be benefits for all. Everyone has to feel that they are being treated fairly. Even groups now intensely at odds can be made partners, of sorts, in an endeavor to make an advanced society.

The program proposes a unique project called the Grand Reconciliation Project designed to allow fair-minded representatives of all identity groups and positions in society to come together to empathize and to find meta-level positions harmonizing opposing ones now. They will learn to emphasize the commonality among people instead of the differences and to make good-faith adjustments towards social harmony. Ultimately, if successful, there will be a consensus on a new social constitution incorporating the new ethos and public values.

The inclusivity theme is designed to develop the collective mentality, provide everybody an opportunity to participate, ameliorate divisiveness among social groups, enhance the social fabric, and release the latent creativity of the little people.

H. Developing Leadership/Bridgers

There will be two types of program leaders–organizational leaders who have executive abilities, traditional management skills, and are influencers; and bridgers. Bridgers are skillful in convincing social groups to overcome trivial differences, exposing invidious mis-framing attempts by those benefiting from divisiveness, and consolidating progressive activists into a single accessible network. They will educate the public about positive social interactions and work to eliminate the power politics among identity groups.

The leaders will have to be team players who except the value of a unified, coherent, and focused program. The National Character Program has to be considered as a *brand*, of sorts, to consolidate all progressives into a single entity. We have to make it *easy* for people to understand the program and to participate in it.

The organizational leaders will build the infrastructure and influence the public about the values of the social ethos. They will build the National Councils, develop the digital communication network, start building the Local Council, administer the Grand Reconciliation Project, appoint the high-level members of the National Council, and more.

Bridgers will reframe existing mindsets to minimize current identity and single position affiliations and create the private versus public citizen attitude distinction we want to emphasize. They will bridge the obsolete categories now in regular use including the Red vs. Blue state, the 1% versus the 99% distinction, and the differences among organized religions.

Organized religions, especially, will be subject to bridging activities to emphasize that they are way more alike than not. It also will be made clear that the doctrinal aspects of religions can be sandboxed, in a sense, from policymaking and governance to the extent that those things are clearly outside of their essential natures. There isn't any good reason for religions to unduly influence education, science, and governance. People need religion but not as a sword or a shield versus others.

Summary–Chapter 6: Values

If the National Character Program is to appeal to anyone it's because it's about values and not just any values but those most likely to appeal to most people in the most meaningful ways. The political-economic context in which we live conditions most of our experiences and outcomes and its values make most of us insecure, distrustful, unhappy, and cynical. That's where our new social ethos comes in, especially the emphasis on BMR–balance, meaning, and respect.

Most people would be more secure, trusting, content, and fulfilled if they lived in a society where there is a healthy balance of private and public interests (Balance), humane considerations are made a big part of capitalism (Meaning), and the good intentions, hard work, and small life outcomes that are major parts of most people's everyday lives are truly valued and respected (Respect.)

For the most part, however, the nation with the most impressive economy is populated by people who are mere producer/buyer cogs in an irrational, heartless, and soulless system. We have an exceptionally economically productive nation with an exceptionally pitiable populace.

When you size up the essential values of balance, meaning, and respect they are not really much to ask for from the social world. After all, we have human needs for meaning and purpose in life other than those imposed upon us by an irrational economic system. And, the vast majority of us are not benefiting from the world's most productive economy to the extent we deserve. Why shouldn't the system serve the people instead of the other way around?

The reasons are that the values of BMR aren't relevant for the logic for our dominant ethos of individualism/capitalism, they run counter to elite interests (and therefore are suppressed or opposed), and (up to now, maybe) there hasn't been a sound vision and plan to achieve those values. That can change, as proposed here.

The BMR values (together with *smart* governance and social relations) are the essential values of the program and we focus on them to make things *easy* for most people to understand the program, and make it accessible. However, the program's set of public values includes other important ones as well. They are: collective fairness; trustworthiness in governance, business, and society; pride in oneself regardless of status; economic efficiency and meaning from a collective's perspective; enhanced respect for reason and science; consideration of multiple perspectives; humility in social conditioning; and tolerance of trivial social differences.

Here is the core set of program values:

New Public Values

1. A balance of private and public citizen values

2. A collective perspective and collective fairness

3. Trustworthiness in government, Big Business, and public society

4. Economic efficiency and meaning from a collective perspective

5. Enhanced respect for science and reason in problem solving

6. Pride in oneself regardless of status

7. Consideration of multiple perspectives

8. Humility based on the limitations of knowledge and social management

9. Tolerance of trivial social group differences

 BMR, Smart governance and social relations

1-3   BMR (as well-described above.)

4. Collective Fairness based on a collective perspective. What is meant by fairness can vary among different people in different situations. For some of the more intense elite members it means getting what they want whenever they want it regardless of the consequences to others because they can do it and get away with it. But for most people, fairness implies a sense of self-esteem and personal dignity, respect for other egos, fair-dealing, and considerations of merit and proportion.

One needs multiple perspectives to analyze and judge fairness standards. But, while there are different standards of fairness, the one which applies most to the program is called "Rawlsian" fairness, based on ideas of philosopher, John Rawls, articulated in his 1971 book "A Theory of Justice." In basic terms, Rawls argued that all societies are run by rules, that any set of specific rules tend to favor certain citizen traits above others, and that whoever makes the rules tends to bias them to benefit *their* traits giving them systemic advantages over everyone else. In other words, the rules matter (a lot) and that it matters (a lot) in who makes them.

Let's, for example, consider a competition between basketballer, Lebron James, and physicist, Stephen Hawking. If the competition was under the rules of basketball, James would have an overwhelming advantage. If the rules were Jeopardy-like questions on nuclear physics they would favor Hawking. Obviously, what set of rules apply to the competition makes all the difference. The same idea applies to society–what set of rules apply and who says so makes the difference.

If we had a set of rules (as we do in America) which favor the aggressive, competitive, self-interested, and wealthiest and were implemented by an elite class (which happens to have that very set of characteristics), those who are public citizen-minded and having fewer resources would be disadvantaged. The system (i.e., the rules of the game) would be *rigged* in favor of the elite.

In the Rawlsian system, the rules would be made by empathetic lawmakers who would take the perspectives of the entire population (the collective) and make rules which would be considerate of *everyone's* characteristics and balance them so no one is disadvantaged from the very beginning. As a rough example, if one of three persons were to slice a pie where the others could pick their slices first, she would likely make three *equal* pieces, thereby leaving no one (including herself) disadvantaged. Social rulemakers, not knowing in advance if they were to be rich or poor, aggressive or not, etc. would likewise design a more neutral set of rules of the game, for the same reason.

Think again of the example above of the military base closing commission whose members attempted to decide base closings based strictly on objective merits, immune from the knowledge and influences of those local congressman, businesses, and communities which would be affected. Closing those bases which had little value to *America* (i.e., the collective) made good sense even though some local people lost jobs, incomes, etc. The process was collectively fair as well as being smart for the nation.

That approach can be generalized to the whole of governance leading to a fairer set of rules of the game not favoring any class or group while being smart for the collective. Not having a collective fairness standard leads to irrational policies for the American nation, the development of an elite class, and unjust economic and political outcomes.

Achieving Rawlsian fairness requires not only a collective perspective but empathy, judgment, and wisdom from the rulemakers. That's one reason that American governance needs the influence of a fair-minded, professional set of leaders and experts having good social character. Those are the people that would populate the national councils which are designed expressly to promote collective fairness and rationality.

5. Trustworthiness in Governance, Business, And Society

A healthy society needs a healthy amount of trust. We want to trust our elected officials, the businesses we transact with, and the institutions and people which comprise the social fabric. Where self-interested individuals dominate, the structural incentives are to compete and exploit and where the context is "Every man for himself" there will be little trust. As we know from current conditions, the populace will learn to be distrusting, insecure, defensive-minded, and cynical. What a lousy way to experience the social world!

In order for there to be collective trust these elements must be present in large degree in government, business, and culture:

-a social ethos containing a collective perspective, including fairness and rationality

-enhanced professionalism in governance, including greater reliance on reason and science in policymaking and decision-making

-democracy in the political sphere where the little people have genuine and effective influence

-governmental officials and policymaking and decision-making in governance "fire-walled," so to speak, from special interests and conflicts of interest

-solid, loophole-free regulation of commercial, consumer, and financial transactions with vigorous enforcement

-personal and institutional leadership emphasizing competence and social character

-a high degree of transparency in governance and business and consumer transactions

-constant monitoring of governmental and business activities by an informal shadow government, including by the Local Council network and private "attorney generals," like class-action attorneys and others.

All of these elements add up to *Credibility* of the cultural system, which creates a more trusting public.

Credibility in culture will come from, among other things: the conditioning effects of the new social ethos, vigorous enforcement of a strong set of legal standards, a universal set of ethical standards, the empowering of the little people in helping make the rules and in enforcing them (we can't let the elite continue to regulate themselves), and a developing social *habit* of good social character.

The program itself, of course, has to earn its own credibility and trust. In addition, the new cultural ethos presents guidance and an opportunity for all of those diminished institutions now which have lost credibility a chance to repair their own reputations.

6. Pride in Oneself Regardless Of Status

Our society places too much emphasis on competition, individual achievement, and on relative status. While those things have their place, there has to be room also for recognition of small life achievements. After all, it is the small life Marys and Johns who comprise most of the population. They don't win major awards and competitions or make the biggest incomes but they teach and coach our children, build and defend our communities, and are responsible for most of our economic value. Why should nearly all Americans accept being considered by the system as inferior and as losers?

The relative status of being the best among others is useful but not the only one for an advanced society. While competition against one another has its benefits we need a new standard of "non"-competition where people compete against their *own potentials*. Those who reach their potentials, regardless of absolute status, should be proud of themselves, recognized by society, and considered winners. Ideally, everyone can be a hero, of sorts.

A smart society would be proud of everyone who is being the best that they can be, regardless of absolute level of achievement. A smart society will recognize the superiority of a standard of having multi-millions of prideful citizens, parents, workers, teachers, etc. to one exulting a mere handful of Nobel Prize winners, Olympic champions, and popular performance artists.

We need strategies to instill pride in people in being the best that they can be, like social encouragement and rewards programs. This type of social conditioning is not much unlike that of teachers, coaches, parents, etc. who apply this kind of motivation to our youths every day. We are just extrapolating the same idea to a national level to everyone, including businesses and other organizations, and making it permanent. It is likely that everyone will benefit in some major ways just interacting with a whole society of prideful people committed to their roles, whether small life status or not.

Some social positions at lower levels of employment, however, may need a subsidy of sorts, to compensate them for their harshness. Nursing home aides or garbage management workers, for example, with extraordinarily challenging job duties can get special compensation or benefits for doing their jobs well. Everyone needs to know that their efforts to be the best that they can be are appreciated. (Note: the capitalist market can't provide these kinds of motivations; it does the *opposite*.)

7. Economic Efficiency And Meaning From A Collective Perspective

You know something is absurd about the incentives of an economic system when it is rational to dump milk or other products to maintain pricing levels even where there are hungry children with unmet needs. You know something is weird when taxpayers pay for unwanted and useless military hardware and unscrupulous manufacturers promote bogus health supplements because they create jobs and sustain communities. (As if we can't find new and better ways of providing jobs and supporting communities using our money in more socially useful ways?) An economic system which values useless products and waste because it provides jobs and profits for some segment of the population is lacking in collective rationality and human meaning.

Furthermore, the incessant artificial manipulation of demand is immoral by most standards as well as wasteful. Some apologists for the system state that the fact that people buy products they don't even want or need do so out of free will and that is justification enough, even though the reality is that consumer buying behaviors are highly manipulated by clever marketers.

Worse, a system which by its own logic has to produce to sell more and more forever *even if the needs of everyone is satisfied in full or suffer a total collapse* is severely irrational and inefficient by every standard (except its own.)

The capitalist market is really a bad environment for BMR. Those things have little measurable value for the system even as they have the highest value for real people. Capitalism is system driven. It has its own imperatives and none of those takes into consideration the value of real human beings. We need a new standard of what economic efficiency means. It means satisfying human needs not system ones. It means stopping production when objective (not manipulated) needs and wants are satisfied. It means having a social purpose for production and marketing decisions.

The object of a new social ethos is to counterbalance that of the individualist/capitalist system to promote a logic satisfying real human values and needs. It will be a big influence on smartening production decisions to eliminate the economic incentives for waste. It will also ensure that neither consumers, taxpayers, or the environment suffer from the externalities caused by business operations which now exploit public resources. We need to hold Big Business accountable for its operations which negatively impact the public by putting compensation for these things into the product pricing itself and not upon the public purse.

Like a lot of developments now in economics, these kinds of changes will be disruptive. And, like many of those actions, it's about time! No question, industries will be economically challenged, jobs will be lost, old ways of doing things will be upset. However, the program has offerings to deal with all of those issues--transitions, soft-landings, retrainings, and more.

We need to start a conversation now about the nature of a new society and especially how economic value is created and allocated among classes and invested in the interests of the collective. The end result will be a smarter, more efficient society, a happier population, and an advanced, 21st-Century nation. That supposedly is what social progress is all about.

Here are some examples of potential substantive changes:

-disruptive reallocation of some industries like the military-industrial complex and the vanity marketing areas. They can evolve into more socially-useful ones. (CEO's who get hundreds of millions of dollars in compensation ought to really earn it by being creative and socially responsible.)

-rationalizing the healthcare system

-making the tax system more transparent and utilizing it as a conditioning method for program policy goals, as well as being fairer among the classes

-reallocating jobs from industries that are not socially useful to those which are, including subsidizing, if necessary, brand-new ones resulting from the "creative destruction" caused by applying smart ideas to old institutions.

8. Enhanced Respect for Reason And Science

Science and technology applications are, of course, drastically altering our material world in (mostly) positive ways. Advancements in the social world however are lagging behind greatly. In the social world they have been limited mostly to sophisticated techniques to convince consumers to buy more and to support political parties and candidates.

Where is the attention to peace making, improving the quality of governance, making people happier, and the like? It's not happening because those things don't pay off under the logic of the capitalist markets which focus on individual interests, not collective ones. A collective perspective, as proposed here, is uniquely capable of incentivizing public citizen values and behaviors drawing upon reason and science to advance the needs and interests of American culture.

The scientific enterprise itself has become less an independent public-spirited endeavor to advance both basic and applied knowledge than a tool of the elite and Big Business to serve their private interests. They fund much of the research focusing their attention to profit-making projects, withhold useful research from the public which is counter to their interests, and entice whole segments of the academic community into conflicts of interest. We need to restore the independence of the scientific enterprise, maintain adequate funding, and direct much of its attention to the needs of the program. We need science to be directed, in part, towards social purposes including flexible employment practices, peacemaking, social conditioning and nudging techniques, group harmony, environmentalism, and solving the problems of group frictions.

Having the benefit of independent science directed towards understanding and solving social problems and baked into the governance processes is the best approach to collective rationality. A professional class of civil servants and academic and expert advisors (under the program's auspices) directly and persistently involved in governance will result in well-researched, deliberated, and wise policymaking and executive decision-making. We have to get away from *upside down* leadership where the worst traits of the public direct the positions and attitudes of our pandering elected officials. (Key members of Congress's Committee on Science, Space, and Technology are evolution and climate change deniers?! What is this?!)

We want to have Big Brains leading our nation rather than Big Mouths! (They know who they are!)

Furthermore, in addition to the lack of smartness in governance, our culture has become burdened by media and popular culture institutions which have contributed to the "dumbing down" of society. Anti-intellectual, purposeless, slacker, and misogynist attitudes have been popularized in many entertainment and other areas. Obviously, there is a market for this material but that ought to be counterbalanced by an attitude exalting the opposite character traits. Think of the 1950's era when cultural material (implicitly, at least) creatively promoted good social character and values. Let's make smartness and good social character appealing again.

We also can't tolerate too much influence by fundamentalists in governance and policymaking. They, too, acquire some of their influence from pandering by elected officials for votes. Their positions and attitudes generally are antithetical to reason and science (and intelligent public policy.) We have to aggressively marginalize them as they can be seriously obstructionist or destructive.

9. Consideration of Multiple Perspectives

Given the many ways different people can frame understandings of nearly everything and the shaping effects of psychology and emotion on beliefs and attitudes it's a wonder that people anywhere can get along on anything. However, fair and nimble-minded people can usually work these differences out. A problem is that too many people have too simple views on important social issues of economics, politics, and social relations and either can't contemplate other perspectives or are manipulated by self-interested parties to be that way for partisan political purposes.

We need to develop an ethos of empathy where multiple perspectives are "visible" and train people in recognizing and understanding other positions and perspectives. We can persuade a lot of people that there are no single worlds or realities out there. We want them to understand the many sides to all stories. That will give people a basis to formulate new, more sophisticated social understandings. (See the material on the Grand Reconciliation Project in Chapter 8.)

Certainly, this is a philosophical issue which may be too complex for many people. Even if it *was* understood completely, it still requires time and effort to discover all those sides to all those stories. Most people can't devote to that kind of effort. That's where fair and nimble-minded leaders and cue-givers play a major role in providing guidance to their constituents and followers. Our leadership will take on the role of explaining multiple perspectives and why empathy, judgment, and wisdom play such a huge role in policymaking and governance.

10. Humility in Social Engineering

Both the lessons of history and the tenets of most political philosophies support the idea that there are limitations on reliance upon reason and science to change society in big ways.

Firstly, the intellectual component of the human psyche is only a small part of life. Values, psychology, emotions, and habit all are highly relevant. Reason has little relevance in some important areas like family and loving relationships, ultimate human purposes, and the like. On the other hand, making significant governance decisions like warmaking, big budgeting expenditures, etc. without (collective) reason is foolhardy. Think of the awful decisions--based on emotions, political pandering, and partisanship-- the United States has made in reaction to the 9-11 incident. There are too many to even list here.

Secondly, history has also shown that overconfidence about the value of science and technology leads to wasteful spending, bad policies, and more. The bigger and more long-standing the problems to be solved the less confidence we ought to have depending on applying mere reason and technology solutions to them.

Nevertheless, there is no question that being *smarter* about these things is better than being dumber. Things are different now in the 21st-Century in that our social management capabilities are way more sophisticated and capable than they were in prior generations. We should be more confident now to try even major disruptive new ideas, technologies, and smartness in policymaking.

Regardless, the National Character Program is quite conservative in its approach and humble in how it expects to operate. These are some of this its essential characteristics:

-it is a nondestructive program; it doesn't intend to tear down institutions or traditions, but to complement them

-it builds incrementally in modular-like format from the top-down and bottom-up without requiring a rigid organizational "blueprint," of sorts; it doesn't have or need a distinct architectural dimension. It will build organically and evolve as needed

-it requires only a modest budget of mostly computer and network equipment supplemented by largely volunteer labor and contributions

-its approach is to change *attitudes* not structural institutions and the like; those things, however, are expected to *evolve* in harmony with the program's new mindset.

-it will be structured in mostly small module components allowing adjustments fairly easily; that means, after testing, if some component or process is not working, the program itself will not fail or be compromised–it will only need repair or supplement

-it will rely on testing methods and strategies in lower profile or exposure areas before moving them to higher more complex levels; there will be a progressive development sort of like a baseball prospect advancing from the minor leagues upwards

-it is flexible and adaptable as it has no rigid and uncompromising principles, other than the very broad concepts of BMR and smart governance and social relations. How those goals get accomplished is very open and accommodating.

11. Insistence on the Quality Of Character

You can think of the ideal program supporter as balancing dual perspectives–the need to defend self-interest and the desire to be responsible to the community she lives in. That person supports the set of public values we are proposing. That person will take pride in (and get respect for) being the best that they can be. Even ordinary Marys and Johns working hard to be the best they can be living the small life will be recognized as social heroes.

12. Tolerance for Trivial Differences

Creating a collective perspective implies that most Americans will see themselves as members of a new social category-public citizens-and members of the American Team.

From the program's macro-level perspective upon the American political-economic system, the only valid social category for our purposes is the private versus public citizen one. That essentially means that a small set of private citizens are opponents, of sort, of the social ethos that the vast majority of Americans will have adopted. Hopefully, the archaic identity and position affiliations that orient most Americans will eventually dissolve. The identity characteristics of social groups of religious, ethnic, region, traditional political partisanship, etc. will be seen as trivial differences, not sufficient enough to act as dividers.

Most importantly, eliminating those trivial differences will provide the large group leverage that the little people need to push back capitalism. There will be little pushback without a collective consciousness. It will also lead to more social harmony as social groups realize that they have way more in common than not and that working together to support the collective interest makes sense for everybody.

We have to be real, however, about these social group differences. They can make sense where competition for scarce resources creates a need to prioritize private interests. They don't, however, make much sense when they are maintained by ignorance, habit, irrational fears, or manipulation by an elite intent on dividing the little people to undercut their group leverage.

Nevertheless, those things won't be easily or quickly overcome. It will take years of promoting efforts in social conditioning, primarily in the areas of education and shared experiences. Fortunately, there are a lot of social science findings to show that these remedies can be effective. We will have to be smart, persistent, and patient.

Summary–Chapter 7: What Do We Want?

There are plenty of Americans who are sick of what we are and don't want to take it anymore. However, they don't know what they can do or they try something which hasn't (and won't) work.

Suggesting blowing up the system doesn't make sense—what does that really mean? And, what do we end up with? Throwing monkey wrenches into the system like the Tea Party does and supporting ridiculously inept presidential candidates like Sarah Palin and Donald Trump may provide some vicarious venting for some but certainly no objective betterment of their lives or a changed society. The Occupy Wall Street movement was impressive in organizing supporters but had no vision at all of a replacement system. And elsewhere, the Arab Spring movements in the Middle East which actually toppled long-standing regimes had no vision of replacement regimes and ended up in worse circumstances.

We must think clearly about what a change of society ought to look like. We already know that it has to build upon (or *around*) what we already have. We know the basic public values we want. But we need to have a detailed and comprehensive program regarding reforming and/or reorienting public and private sector institutions and processes, specific ethical guidelines for government and Big Business, ways to condition new cultural mores, ways to mobilize the little people, and the like. What changes? How? When? How long will it take? Will it last? We can summarize the essentials of what we want to BMR and *smart* governance and social relations.

However, we have to have what organizational types call *operational* elements which means a comprehensive, detailed program which guides people how to apply our principles to their everyday situations. Here are some components of an operational program in four categories: finance, economics, politics and democracy, and society and culture.

What Do We Want?

A. *Financial*

Regulations protecting the little people

Vigorously law enforcement and penalties

Credible accounting systems

Global finance coordination

Fiscal responsibility and transparency

B. *Economics* -

Reallocation of spending to socially   useful things

Rationalize the healthcare system

Rationalize governmental administration

Reform the tax system and utilize it better

Reallocation of the capital/labor value ratio

Streamline business operations

Eliminate locality whipsaws

Enhance workers' health, safety, and work-family balances

Stop high-level leadership compensation gouging................................. (Cont'd.)

Rigorous consumer protection

Enhanced respect for the environment

C. Politics and Democracy

Sandbox government and its officials from special interest influences

Enact electoral, campaign, and apportionment rules to increase democracy

Rationalize the entire electoral process nationally

Raise the level of candidate quality requirements

Eliminate the structural impediments to third-party organization

Require good social character in leadership including equalizing official compensation to constituents

Raise the level of public discourse

Revert leadership to guiding and educating constituents instead of pandering to them

Professionalize the executive appointment process

Set special bumps before the President in waging war

Enhance privacy rights   (Cont'd.)

D. Socio-economic and Cultural

Raise the level of social trust

Conditioning programs for public citizen attitude

Get a habit of moderating the private/ public citizen tension

Build out the social fabric

Reduce the role of religion in the public sphere

Grow inclusivity

Increase environmental awareness, especially regarding social goals

A. Finance

1. The financial system has to be **sufficiently regulated** to protect the little people from the consequences of the excessive risk taking, short-term perspectives, moral hazards, and manipulations of the elite class. We shouldn't care what individuals do with their own money as long as they don't create systemic problems affecting the rest of us and cause damage to the innocent. Of course, that regulation can't be designed by the elite themselves. Our professionals (as in the Policy and Problem-Solving and Planning Councils) can readily design a scheme which protects the public and the collective interest.

The elite will squawk about impinging on their freedoms, constraining their competitiveness and profit (Heavens no!), and bogus lamenting of "Loss of jobs," but that is just too bad! Something has to give! We either protect the innocent or allow the aggressive, self-interested to screw us again and again. (As for the loss of jobs, we have answers for that–see below.)

2. The financial system regulation has to be supported by **vigorous enforcement.** Needless to say, the elite can't design the enforcement mechanisms either, nor influence their operations. We need loophole-free rules and sandboxed enforcement personnel immune from elite manipulations. The enforcement will be costly for taxpayers as we will have to counter the legions of lawyers, lobbyists, and other cronies employed by the elite. Nevertheless, the short-term costs will easily be offset by the mid-long-term savings for consumers and taxpayers. There also will be deeply-affecting social benefits pertaining to fairness and trust.

Penalties and enforcements also have to have a deterrent quality not present now. Just check the records for the criminal and bad acts of the elite class, especially the multitude of corporate recidivists. Under the circumstances we have now even the worst corporate miscreants get away with bad acts much more consequential than those of thousands of street criminals combined.

Punishment of this kind of white-collar crime ought to match or exceed that of robbers of convenience stores as the negative consequences are so much greater. The effects of the 2008 Great Recession resulted in multi-millions of lost jobs, homes, pensions, and more, adding up to multi-billions of dollars, as well as crushing lives, dreams, and beliefs in the "American way." We need to be as hard, or harder, on those miscreants as they are upon the little guys who have to sell marijuana on the streets to support their families. And, we have to be especially hard on the corporate recidivists. No more nickel and dime financial penalties and no more country club confinements for the few actively prosecuted. Attica for those blue-chip perps! Maybe *that* will change their behavior.

3. The ratings and auditing companies culpable for the egregious misrepresentations of financial circumstances of public and private sector entities in the Great Recession exposed in a separate way the severe consequences of letting the elite regulate themselves. The level of social and personal irresponsibility was astonishing and outrageous. The system was permeated with conflicts of interest, incompetence, manipulation, and incentives to compromise truth and accountability. Not surprisingly, after the hectic game of financial musical chairs it was the taxpayers and the little guy innocents who were left without support.

The entire auditing systems of both the private and public sectors need **credibility and accessibility.** It may not be feasible to much *reform* the system of private institutions which maintain, evaluate, and distribute financial data. It may take new, perhaps public institutions to provide the honest services needed by participants in the financial sphere. We can make those engaged there fund these institutions through transactional fees, perhaps. We'll insist upon responsible ethical standards for all participants. We can have our own professionals create universal templates for what needs to be reported and how.

This concept of honest, accessible reporting of financial circumstances has to apply to governments, as well. We need credible institutions to monitor, evaluate, and disclose public finances, beyond just the oversight of the informal Local Council. We can't tolerate any longer "back room" financing shenanigans, misleading data, "off-budget" items, and income/expense projections from politicians and special interests based on ridiculously optimistic assumptions that they blithely foist upon the public. Governments at all levels should regularly produce profit/loss and net worth statements and similar financial disclosures in an accessible form to the public. The public needs to know clearly what is going on with its money.

4. We have a truly global financial system and what we do in America will **have to be coordinated** with the rest of the world to a great degree. Much of the conceptual infrastructure among nations is already in place. Rational, professional regulation of the financial world will require all (financially-developed) nations to adapt to rules supporting a collective perspective. That means, among other things, collective rationality, protecting the little people from the elite, upgrading inadequate established practices on global labor and environmental standards, and more.

Up until now, it's been the bare-knuckled aggressive capitalism of corporate America which has dominated economic behavior and held back much of the progressive developments necessary for advanced societies. The European Union may present a model of how this kind of progressive, multi-national cooperation can work.

5. Classical conservatives have long pointed out that liberal democratic governments can't be trusted to be really **fiscally responsible.** There is some truth to that, as it is too tempting for elected officials to satisfy their own interests (or those of special interests) with funds not their own. They spend with borrowed money, implement programs which are not fiscally-sound in an amortization sense, and worse. Even those recognizing the long-term negative consequences of unsound fiscal decisions have little incentive to refrain from them as these consequences will be *somebody else's* problem when they occur.

None of this means that government or its revenues necessarily ought to be minimized. The logic doesn't require smaller government only *better* government, guided by standards of fiscal responsibility (developed by the Policy and Problem-Solving and Planning Councils.)

Beyond just the truthful, accessible accounting described above we also need a set of reforms of government (some will be described below) to immunize governments from the undue influences of special interests, to sandbox officials to maintain honesty and credibility, to have high standards of professionalism and competence for our officials, and to condition our representatives to act with good social character. Much of that can be derived from the social ethos which is at the heart of the program.

Of course, government isn't to be held to the exact same standards as those in the private sector. It has special responsibilities as representative of the collective–guarantor or lender of last resort (in some cases), spending whatever is necessary to defend national interests (as in wartime, etc.), and the like. But, generally, governments should be as fiscally responsible as individuals and private organizations everywhere else. That means that budgets will be balanced, pensions will be adequately funded, tax rates imposed that make sense for the collective good, and the like.

B. Economics

1. The most significant thing that we can do economically is to stop spending money on things we don't need and **redirect that spending** to those things we *do* need and want. We spend nearly half the federal budget, at least, on the military and national defence. Much of that is spent on expensive unwanted and useless hardware. Special interests and their lobbyists and marketers promote waste and useless buying, relying on easily manipulated government officials. On the other hand, we have well-recognized social needs to update public infrastructure, promote alternative energy industries, sincerely address the lower class disadvantages in the economic world, and more.

An intellectually-sound (collective) budget would have a significantly different allocation of governmental spending. Accomplishing this would likely mean reorienting whole big industries, like the military-industrial complex, and others. Why not set out new public objectives, give these industries a long transition program to adjust to the new realities, and provide soft landings for all affected parties? Then they would be repositioned as socially worthwhile participants in a collective endeavor.

The disruptions here in this reorientation of specific socially-adverse businesses (as in other industries) may imply a need for a major reconsideration of traditional employment practices. Workers may need to be way more flexible in job roles, locations, and company affiliations. However, with modern technology and other means, including legal reforms of benefit programs and the like, these adjustments may ultimately work nicely for everyone (except for those absolutely rigid in their habits–we can't please everyone!)

2. Rationalizing the health care system towards the model already in place in nearly every other developed nation is truly a no-brainer. (As we know, we don't have a collective perspective and reason alone is insufficient to motivate a lot of people. Even if it weren't, we still don't have an institution(s)–a brain in government--to operate in that way.)

The rationalization can reduce costs, improve health outcomes, and eliminate most of the hated/dreaded *process* of paying for health services. Another benefit will be a rationalization of the disdained medical malpractice area which can be characterized as highly inefficient and unfair, litigation-oriented, and stressful and misdirected for health professional and patient relationships. This is truly an easy fix (à la the workers compensation model, or similar) which will provide more and fairer distribution of benefits, eliminate litigation, enhance the professional-patient relationship, and ease psychological tensions of both those making the errors and those on the receiving end. (We will have soft landing programs for the trial lawyers and others impacted by this change.)

Of course, extending healthcare benefits to everyone is a *substantive* decision to be made by American citizens as a policy choice. The program itself doesn't take a position on such an issue but only wants to apply reason and a collective perspective to solving a major cost problem and an irritation to nearly everyone.

3. Rationalizing governmental administration: In the Internet Age with advanced communication and management tools and a lingering concern about the costs of government why do we need 6200 or so separate governmental entities in New York State *alone*? Why do we need fifty state DMV's each with their own sets of officials, budgets, and rules? And, in a mostly homogenized 21st-Century America, why even have fifty separate states? We can rationalize structures and processes (relying on expert templates), cut budgets, and make life easier for an advanced society where 18th-Century artificial boundaries and ways of doing things are meaningless and wasteful.

We can consolidate governmental jurisdictions, make universal rules and practices for lots of subject areas, and simplify life for nearly everyone, as well as saving a lot of money. Accomplishing this will require disrupting the legion of local fiefdoms acting as job placement repositories for local political elites and their cronies. The strong social *habit* of such traditional institutions will also have to be addressed. As they say, there can be no omelettes without breaking eggs!

4. Reform the tax system and utilize it better: Nearly everyone wants to reform the tax system but not many have the best interests of the collective in mind or the sense of smartness we want to add to governance. Most people want reform to cut taxes indiscriminately or their just own for self-interested reasons. From the collective's point of view, here is what tax system reform should look like:

-make it fairer by eliminating the outright giveaways to special interests like the low-rate carried interest concept applicable only to Wall Street brokerage firms

-make the rates way more progressive. This will *not* (according to studies) reduce incentives to work and invest like some say but will help minimize the unjust economic outcomes produced by the system. Another major advantage to this approach is that it will eliminate the well-intended but poorly conceived and futile attempts to tinker with a whole lot of economic aspects of society to address unjust inequality, like caps on executive pay, the market flaws giving celebrities and sports stars incomes way beyond rational levels, and a host of other incoherent adjustments to trying to remedy elite excesses. We can just leave the economy to run itself as it has while *extracting the surplus value by the progressive rates*. This means hands off the economy, as many conservatives and individualist desire, but achieving collective fairness through simple tax rate progressivity.

-re-evaluation from a collective's perspective of all the subsidy and social conditioning programs now in place in the tax rules, like the mortgage interest deduction and similar others, which may have outlived their utility and now just distort coherent economic decisions and add to the unfairness among groups (e.g., homeowners versus renters.) Let a collective perspective (as determined by the Policy and Problem-Solving Council) evaluate and fix these things.

-certainly we need to step up enforcement in all aspects. That means loophole-free rules, sufficient and vigorous enforcement of the rules, and new ideas on dealing with multi-national tax matters. Not only are our generations-old, jurisdiction-based schemes inadequate in a global economy, the ease by which thousands of Big Businesses evade taxation by having (bogus) presences in tax-friendly foreign lands is an insult to hard-working stiffs who *do* pay their fair share.

-remake the incentives and conditioning policy provisions of the tax system more relevant to the social ethos we want to create. That means using the system more to target and condition public citizen activities. (This implies full and accessible disclosure to the public--via templates--of what activities are being subsidized and why.)

-an understanding among those involved in public policy that the nation will raise revenues to match its needs and that lower taxes as an "election campaign" position without consideration of *value* received is just ignorant and foolish. The tax rate ought to meet revenue needs regardless of absolute level. Understand with this that new professionalism and collective rationality elements will minimize waste and giveaways to private citizens. That might make paying taxes feel less of a looting and more of a welcome duty.

5. Reallocation of the capital/labor value ratio: This may be the most significant economic issue. Economists routinely measure how much economic value is allocated over time to capital and labor. This ratio is meant to determine the merits of respective contributions to economic value but mostly a matter of fundamental class fairness. It has varied over centuries but has improved greatly in favor of the elite over the last handful of generations and not because of merit but because the elite are more aggressive now in grabbing an excessive share.

Experts and policymakers (with a collective perspective) can establish in connection with *class negotiation* (see the Grand Reconciliation Project discussion in Chapter 8) a fair ratio which would, at a minimum, allow the lower classes to have a reasonable standard of living and an opportunity to advance on merit, sustain a large and vibrant middle class, and still have a good deal of economic value left over to satisfy the elite (except for the most greedy and arrogant of them–too bad!)

The ratio can be maintained in two ways–the most efficient and practical way is by utilizing the tax rates and targeted subsidies to adjust the allocation ratio. We then supplement that by tweaks to aspects of the economy like the minimum wage level, overtime compensation and the like, and reduction in competitive disadvantages to the lower classes in education, family life, and social support.

This economic "partnership," so to speak, would mimic the relationship in the professional sports world among the owners of NBA, NFL, NHL teams and their player unions. The collective bargaining agreements between owners and players' unions establish a fair and relatively permanent split of revenues. Once those ratios were set, most financial conflict has been avoided. The parties thrive now to *grow the partnership* rather than *fight* perpetually over the allocation ratio. Frictions are mostly over relatively minor non-economic issues.

In any case, however, utilizing the tax system and statutory regulation of the economy will likely be insufficient to maintain the allocation ratio. These mechanisms rely nearly totally on the political system (which we intend to reform--see below) but which will likely be insufficient in itself to pushback the capitalists. We need the little people to enforce pushback in workplaces, in the business and consumer spheres, and elsewhere.

In the last century or so, little people saw improvements pretty much only because of the major unions. Either they were union members themselves or benefited indirectly from the uplifting of compensation and employee rights levels throughout the economy. The rise of the middle class in the 1930's through the 1980's was the result mostly of the economic and political power of those unions.

The unions now have become crushed with the consequent direct decline of the middle class and the even more serious deterioration of the lower class. The unions today have been demonized and deliberately diminished by the elite, they have undercut their own credibility themselves by evolving into special interests instead of collective worker and societal interest proponents as they had been decades ago, and they have developed (in some cases) reputations for overreaching, cronyism, and corruption.

Nevertheless, *reformulated and rebranded* unions will likely be the most effective way for the little people to push back upon the private citizen/capitalist system. They have learned pushback-type techniques from experience, they know how to mobilize support, and they have resources. They now need *credibility,* re-establishing themselves as collective, *general interest* entities working for the progressive interests of all workers, organized or not, and the general public.

Mostly, they have to stop acting like special interests. They have to support progressive social development and public citizen values generally. In the mid-20th-Century they supported *all* workers, supported Social Security and other progressive national programs, and provided leadership in the civil rights movement, among other activities. They can return to that tradition and earn back the all-important *credibility* they need. It will take time to reformulate themselves as rebranded organizations but they will be the biggest asset to our pushback efforts.

Not all employee-related pushback, however, has to come from organized labor. Informal groups of independent workers in all kinds of industries can draw upon templates of "Best Office And Shop Environments, etc." and similar tools designed (by the Support Council) to provide guidance and perspectives to management and labor of expectations in the workplace regarding BMR. Workers knowing of other places in their industry/region which *have* harmonized with BMR principles can put informal pressures of various sorts upon their bosses as to why *they* are not up to standards. The practical, social, and moral pressures alone of even unorganized workers may be effective in some situations.

All of these efforts will be supplemented by legal reforms supporting unionization, workplace rights, and progressive work-family balances.

6. Streamline business operations: It may be helpful to businesses to strip off from them the social-type responsibilities many have now, like providing health care insurance and the like. Firstly, businesses may work better and be more competitive globally by focusing on their essential business plans. Secondly, those benefits and services may be provided more efficiently and at lower cost by governmental-structured entities. The net effect may be better, cheaper, more consistent worker benefits and more revenue available to businesses to increase wages and benefits for their workers.

7. Eliminate the locality whipsaws: Whether by statute or otherwise the ability of businesses and sports franchises to extort public value for their own private interests must stop. They shop their jobs and prestige to desperate localities everywhere to obtain tax breaks, free public services, and other goodies. Not only is this practice costly to communities but it is an outrageous insult to the collective interest. It highlights the private citizen attitude and increases public cynicism while also contributing to corruption in government.

8. Enhance worker health and safety protection practices and work-family balances:
Aligned with, but different, than adjusting the capital/labor value ratio, are worker rights to be treated as human beings and not merely as human capital. That implies sufficient consideration for those things implying human meanings–family, sick, vacation, and similar leaves; flex time; sufficient and regular work hours; right to be "off the clock" free of 24/7 work duties; and digital tethering and supervision, and the like. There must be a work/person balance everywhere at all times.

This issue ought to apply at *all* levels of employment. Even when high-level corporate policy, for example, allows ample leave time for a CEO, workplace mores undercut those policies as they are not *sincerely* offered. The hard-core capitalist ethos subjugates every aspect of human meaning to its own imperatives and many employees incur negative consequences regarding promotions, bonuses, and more just for trying to have a human balance of interests in their lives. Even high-level workers interested in having quality family relationships have an interest to join in pushback against the prevailing ethos. A healthy, advanced society does not allow work to constantly trump family and community.

9. Stop high-level leadership compensation gouging: The wide-open gouging opportunities for CEO's of corporations, universities, and of non-profit organizations has to be curtailed. It is exceedingly easy for these folks to set their own compensation levels without much constraint (i.e., higher and higher) using other people's money. This tends to drive up costs throughout the organization and unfairly distorts status levels at the expense of stockholders, students, and contributors. This is, like the whipsaw activities noted above, an insult, a driver of cynicism, and contributes to distrust of authority organizations. Perhaps the worst consequence is the escalation of college costs inhibiting more and more potential lower-class students from getting higher educations.

10. Rigorous consumer protections: "Consumer beware!" is no longer an acceptable premise. That has to be turned around. Not only will deception and manipulation of the consumers have to stop but businesses and marketers which do not adapt to BMR principles will be subject to pushback until they comply (or go under.) This means that the multiple ways in which consumers transact with businesses will have to be on fair and open terms. That means minimum warranties, at least, with easy claim administration, accessible lender and sale disclosures, honesty in product descriptions, and the like, all vigorously enforced by legal authorities and/or empowered class-action lawyers and self-help means.

Templates for best practices and documents will be designed and promoted by our experts and professionals (i.e., the Support Council) to make it easy for everyone to comply. If honesty in business models doesn't work for some owners those businesses deserve to go under!

11. Enhanced Respect for the environment: As we are using up or destroying environmental capital, the long run may be unpleasant for future generations. Taking an intelligent approach to conserving our resources including mid-long-term perspectives makes good sense. We need to condition everyone to understanding the vulnerability of environmental capital (and the long-term economy) to irresponsible, unthinking, and avoidable human activity. We would like such consideration to become a social habit. We will have Planning and Support Councils to help with that.

Big Business externalities will be addressed by regulation and guidance from best practices templates. Furthermore, as part of smart governance, we want to diminish the influence of those people in a position of authority (e.g., members of congressional committees and the like) who are ignorant, panderers, and/or partisan politics biased. The overall social ethos emphasizing smartness in governance and professionalism in operations may work to address this problem.

C. Politics and Democracy

We need more and better democracy. We do have to acknowledge the preferred place of the elite in steering the Ship of State, so to speak, but not its near exclusivity. The lower classes need more influence in governance, elections, and especially policy outcomes. Here are some ideas on how this may happen:

-close off the openness of government to special interests

-eliminate the Iron Triangles

-sandbox elected officials from undue influences and conflicts of interest. That may require exclusivity of public (or controlled) financing of campaigns, etc.

-enact electoral rules minimizing the influence of wealth and special interests

-rationalize the entire electoral process nationwide, perhaps promoting templates of best election practices relating to voter registration, administration of voting, shorter campaign periods, longer terms of office, etc.

-rationalizing the district apportionment system to minimize bias and enhance collective values, including updating the 18th-Century congressional apportionment structures

-emphasize candidate and official resumes and qualifications rather than accept near empty criteria sets for office

-(perhaps) eliminate legal and structural impediments to third-party organizations

-require and enforce the values of professionalism competence, and social character of public servants at all levels of government

-bring the practical work environment of our elected officials (especially their perquisites and benefits) closer to the level of the typical American worker. If the Marys and Johns get no pensions, lousy health coverage, and the like, public servants get the same

-public discourse levels have to be raised. We have to emphasize the function of smartness in governance (supported by best practice templates and the like) to raise the quality public discourse on elections, policymaking and governmental operations. This consideration is aimed at the professional politicians themselves (especially the major parties) which have become mostly irresponsible and the news media which has prioritized entertainment values and (invalidly) given equal attention to alternative partisan policy positions regardless of quality and relevance. (For example, 2012 presidential candidate, Herman Cain's, "999" program ought not be given the same attention as more truly intellectual positions of more serious people.) This means that the media has to become more professional and socially responsible. (If they refuse or can't, we will create our own professional news media–see Chapter 8.)

-highlight the social quality of true leadership where the better informed, experienced, and qualified actually educate and guide their constituents and followers instead of the upside down pandering we tolerate now where the worst of the electorate dictate positions *to* feckless candidates.

-public discourse in elections and policy discourse should emphasize what the serious, committed voters need and not what the elite want to tell (manipulate) us.

-rationalize the executive apportionment process to make it less partisan in the selection of professional and technical personnel like judges and others

-set speed-bumps before the President on waging war and engaging in military actions

-create an effective institution (perhaps within the shadow government) to constrain the post-9/11 outright disregard by our government for privacy rights. This disregard is used as a ploy to assert the most significant surveillance and control of Americans ever conceived instead of merely protecting us from terrorists and other bogeymen. The trade-offs between security and privacy have become highly biased against privacy expectations.

Some of these proposals will require amendments to the U.S. Constitution. Although the amendment process is difficult, a carefully designed package of proposals authorizing implementation of National Character Program ideas may happen once the credibility of the movement has been established. We want to ensure that the package is humbly limited to smart governance proposals and not become an opportunity for partisans of all kinds pushing for the addition of substantive provisions, like new rights to jobs, housing, abortion denials, etc. We don't want to try to vote them in under the individual/special interest, identity-based political processes which are a symptom of what is wrong with America. Good things will come from the proper *approaches* to substantive issues based upon smartness.

D. Sociological and Cultural

Social trust

 Perhaps the most significant sociological/cultural element we want to promote is that of social trust. Our new ethos of a collective perspective where cooperation and harmony are emphasized counterbalances the individualist/capitalist ethos of every man for himself, i.e., distrust of everybody, as a matter of practical philosophy.

Many of the components itemized in the sections above will contribute to the new sense of social trust– the National Council representing the collective and good social character as a sort of role model, regulation of the financial system, major economic changes, vigorous enforcement of rules and laws, a brain and professionalism in governance, and more, will create a basis for a big surge in social trust.

Other components under this section include: extensive and permanent social conditioning, consistent attention to the dual-citizen concept, building out of the social fabric, reducing the role of religion in the public sphere, inclusivity, and long-term environmental/existential awareness.

Social conditioning to the public citizen attitude

As we are persistently conditioned to be good consumers and workers, we need to counterbalance that with conditioning to the public citizen attitude. The conditioning will be broadly-based and permanent. There may be many different strategies and programs involving educational curricula, rewards programs, role model and cue-giving strategies, popular media materials, and maybe most usefully, templates on how to be a Good Citizen, Parent, Businessman, Public Servant, and many more.

No one should assume that people develop the knowledge of what those roles mean, much less take them to heart and make them habits, simply from daily experience. In fact, they likely will be conditioned by marketers to be the opposite as none of those roles fit the conceptual design of capitalism.

Private/public duel-citizen concept

Once people are comfortable with the private vs. public citizen categorization they can decide for themselves which attitude fits them better, or what kind of balance works for them. Ideally, most people will understand and feel that a healthier balance is preferred. Having only the two attitudes makes it easy for people to fit into one or the other. They can ease away from all of the other social categories which will then feel mostly irrelevant, like ethnicity, religion and partisan affiliations, and others.

People can't, however, get beyond the *constant tension* between the two attitudes but at least the public citizen one will be reinforced by the social conditioning programs. There may be a lot of practical role changes:

-Businesses will consider the interests of all stakeholders in their endeavors–owners, workers, the community, the environment, future generations, etc.–instead of only shareholders

-Employers will deal with their employees in a more humane manner regarding work-family balances, etc.

-Public officials will be secure in focusing on professional performance and the collective interest

-Popular cultural producers will incorporate public citizen themes into their materials

-The news media will re-establish credibility for quality and professionalism

-Etc.

Building out the social fabric

While some people may now see the American social fabric as a colorful and textural mosaic, it is really more like a clothing repository where all the clothing items are strewn all over the floor of a large warehouse. Instead of coherence and connectedness, there is separateness and dysfunction. Given the social group perspective, however, of private vs. public citizen, all of the social identity and position groups in America will be viewed as mostly irrelevant and abrasive to a healthy social fabric.

The inclusivity theme works in a lot of positive ways. It:

-clarifies the significance of the two major social groups–private and public citizens

-organizes public citizens (especially the little people) into a single group, via the Local Council, together with its political and consumer leverages

-minimizes the trivial discriminations and frictions among the newly obsolete but still active social groups

-strengthens connecting at the grassroots level up through the higher-level organization. This will facilitate problem solving and community building by providing "ownership" of sorts by locals of their own issues first, while eventually building up larger communities.

Reducing the role of religion in the public sphere

While the approach to this topic threatens to be controversial *it should not be* for those thinking clearly about the essence of the issues. Religion is intended to soften the fear and dread which comes from cognition of mortality and personal responsibility for one's own life in a cruel (and often purposeless) world. That function *is a very good thing* for those who are comforted by it (and not everyone is, or needs it.)

Given this understanding, religion is a personal matter only! (notwithstanding the separate but non-essential benefits which come from an organized social grouping.) Given that idea, all the other aspects of religions are superfluous. There is no reason for them to have a position on science, governance, medicine, and the like as these are really *non-jurisdictional* elements, in a sense.

Nevertheless, hardly anyone seemingly sees religion in this way which may account for why there are doctrinal and other frictions among separate religions and the counter productive consequences of religions holding back education, medicine, science, and smart governance. We want to see a sandboxing of religion to its important essences.

Grow inclusivity

First, we minimize most other social groupings and promote a private/public citizen one. That works primarily for the political function of the program to leverage the little people for pushback.

Secondly, we encourage social harmony by emphasizing commonalities over trivial differences, minimizing social frictions. That result in itself will be worthwhile but it will also take away one of the most important elite strategies of control by dividing the little people and getting them to fight among themselves thereby dissipating their political leverage.

There can be a whole lot of strategies to overcome the ignorance and habit motivations for current social differences:

-Educational programming in schools, workplaces, government, and especially popular cultural media (think of the TV shows All in the Family and the Cosby Show, etc.)

-Proactive outreach of each social group to all the others via invitations to open houses, cultural events, exchanges of various sorts, etc.

-And more.

Broad-based environmental awareness

This means way more than mere awareness of conservation of natural resources and stewardship of the natural world. If the smart approach to governance works like we want, there will be major disruptions in the broad sphere of human activities. Of course, there will need to be a broad-based dialogue about how to adjust to these things. Answers now would be premature as we are decades away from any of the consequences, but we should at least draw up a list of things to consider:

-What will be the elements of a soft landing when major industries are gone (or reoriented)?

-What do we do with the multi-millions of people without jobs as the traditional economy has no places for them?

-How are we to handle the philosophical change in the economy from one where the system requires perpetual buying and producing to one where we accept that once all human needs and wants are satisfied it doesn't make sense to continue to produce and consume more?

-Can we set goals for the collective, like global peace, universal economic security, and the like, when traditionally we have not set *any* since we have an individualist attitude that everybody sets their own goals entirely independent of their ties to the society?

These are indeed weighty existential questions which need to be brought to the attention of the public and a start made on what the answers may be.

Summary–Chapter 8: The Program

Close to *nothing*! That's what you have when you have only these elements: a broad-recognition that most Americans are being treated unfairly by a rigged political-economic system, a good analysis of what/who is responsible, a great deal of "heart" among millions of Americans interested in social change, and resources like intelligence, money, technology, skills, and creativity.

Now, let's add these additional elements: a sound vision and practical plan of what significant social change in America looks like and how to get it (i.e., the "Story"); broad distribution of the basics of the vision and plan; a communications network including websites, online collaboration tools, and social media; a focused, accessible network mobilizing a lot of the little people creating a unique level of leverage from their numerical voting power and consumer weightiness; and a long-term commitment by a lot of people.

Together these two sets of elements add up to a potentially successful social movement that can affect major social change and result in an advanced 21st-Century America. The structural and process elements of the movement are presented below. How to effect them will be discussed in the next chapter.

An ambitious vision like the one proposed here can only be a sketch as we are talking about a type of historical movement rarely experienced, like the overthrow of feudalism in the 14th-Century, the rise of democratic ideals in the late 18th-Century, and (on a more modest scale) the civil rights, feminist, and gender orientation movements of recent times.

No program of this comprehensiveness and ambition can be without some vagueness and uncertainties. But its feasibility is enhanced by its non-ideological nature, its focus mostly on attitudes and mindsets and not on replacing well-entrenched institutions, and its harmony with so many elements already in place in contemporary America. Those include increasing "disruptiveness" in industries and in the old ways of doing things, globalism, increasing populism, the presence of legions of progressive activist organizations already implementing *some* of its ideas, and more.

The program is an analysis of much of what is wrong with America (for the little people) and a synthesis of ideas, values, and projects already present and active but lacking much influence or effectiveness. What the program offers is a comprehensive vision of what is possible, a focus on a small set of basic values and a new approach to governance, and the kind of accessibility needed to mobilize those millions of people needed to make it happen. (Note: the program doesn't need everyone to participate–it may work with as few as 15 to 30% of Americans to support it.)

1. The Structures of the program

The Program will have six national councils: a National Council, Planning, Policy and Problem-Solving, Information, Support, and Local councils, and a National University.

The national councils will be led mostly by a combination of high-profile influencer types, "Big Project" producers, top-level academics and professional experts, progressive activist leaders, and technological design gurus. They will be populated in the middle levels primarily by a whole lot of activist organizations either existing or new, while the Local Council especially will be comprised mostly of ordinary Marys and Johns empowered by accessible technology and a newly acquired attitude of entitlement to BMR.

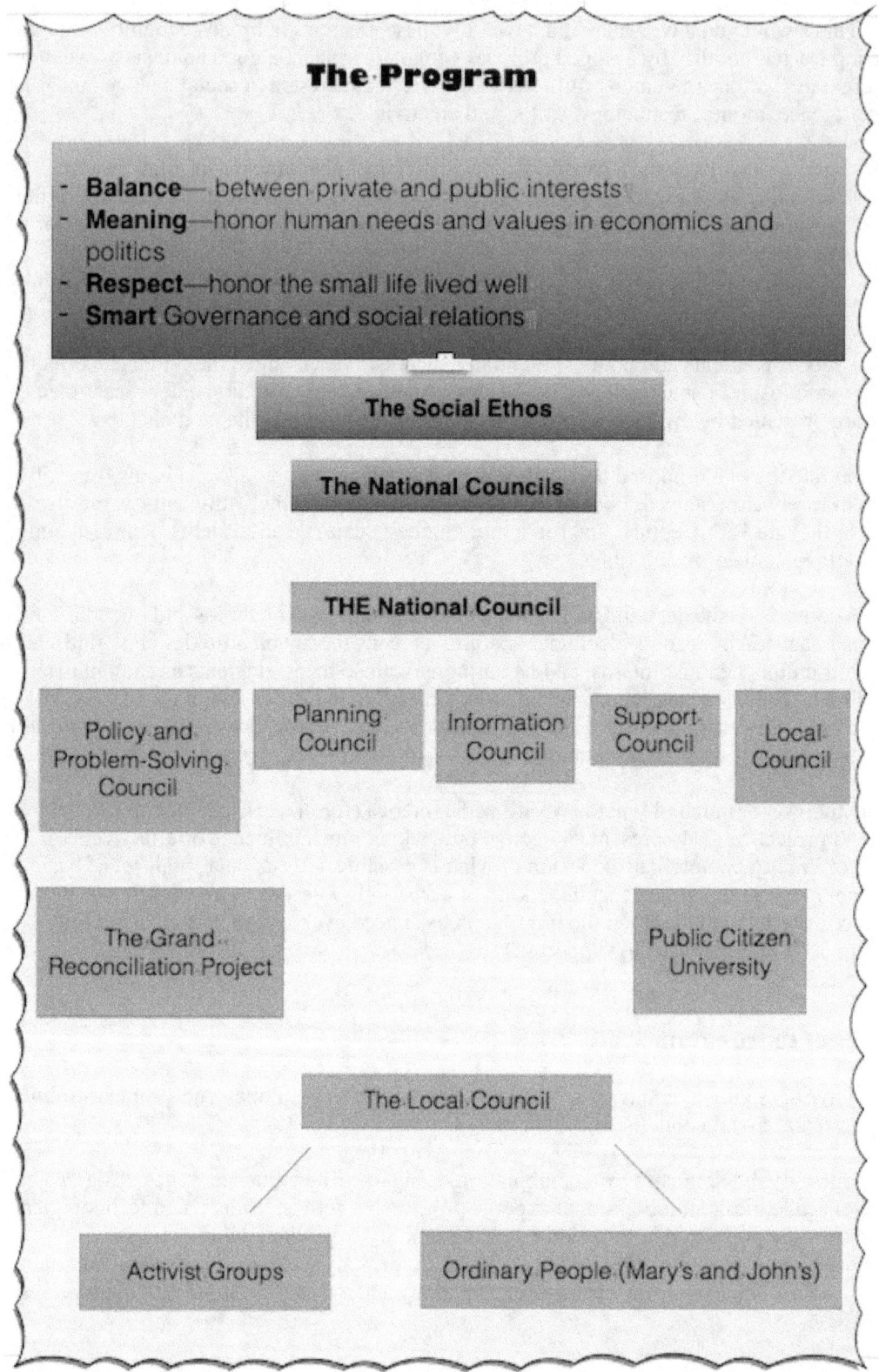

The Program

- **Balance**— between private and public interests
- **Meaning**—honor human needs and values in economics and politics
- **Respect**—honor the small life lived well
- **Smart** Governance and social relations

The Social Ethos

The National Councils

THE National Council

Policy and Problem-Solving Council

Planning Council

Information Council

Support Council

Local Council

The Grand Reconciliation Project

Public Citizen University

The Local Council

Activist Groups

Ordinary People (Mary's and John's)

The absolute key to the program will be the unity of all of these discrete structural elements under a single "brand," so to speak. That brand will have a narrow focus on BMR and public values, and accessibility to all those who may want to participate. In actuality, while the movement will be conceived as one brand, its internal structure will have multiple components as it will be organically-composed, built from both the top-down and bottom-up simultaneously, with no defined order of completion. Its operations will be organized with a communications infrastructure/network connecting everyone together.

A. The National Council

This council will be the face and the soul of the program comprised of a large handful (30-40) of high-profile people having the respect of large segments of the American public. They will have these characteristics: great integrity, fair and nimble mindedness, team player personalities, charismatic and inspirational personalities, and wisdom and judgment. They will embody the good social character and social ethos of the program.

The members of Council will be representative of all of the major *perspectives* in America related to economics, politics, and social relations. They will *not* represent specific interest, identity, or affinity groups. The idea is to make sure that the perspectives of all groups and positions in society are part of an inclusive membership body standing for a *collective*. Those multiple perspectives will be molded into an overall collective perspective representing all Americans and an American nation.

In some ways, these members will be like U.S. Supreme Court justices having ultimate authority over ultimate principles. However, instead of ruling on legal questions brought to them by mostly private litigants, the Council will take positions on macro-level economic, political, and social matters which will be reflected in the new social ethos–BMR, public values, and smart governance and social relations. Those values, perhaps, will be formalized in a new *social* constitution, of sorts. That constitution will be developed by a different set of participants intending to renovate our basic governance principles and processes. (See below for discussion of the Grand Reconciliation Project.)

The Council will view America from a big picture, macro-level and evaluate how government, Big Business, and other aspects in society comply with the principles of the new ethos and social constitution. They will be primarily responsible to "sell" the recommendation and Action Plans of the other councils to the public. They will act as a sort of bully pulpit (having no official legal authority) but having considerable breadth of interests and a unique perspective and credibility. That credibility will derive from the good social character that the Council represents, the inclusivity of multiple perspectives, an emphasis on a collective perspective and fairness, and the *insistence* upon major social change, something nearly everyone wants. The Council may earn credibility no other (quasi) governmental institution has ever had.

Beyond standing as the primary symbol of the new movement, the National Council will draw upon research (from other councils), evaluate, give opinions, and make recommendations to the public about matters within its jurisdiction (sort of like opinions of the U.S. Supreme Court.) The Council's positions will be enforced by its symbolic leadership, moral authority, credibility, and enforcement-like capabilities directing the pushback functions of the program (those of the Local Council, especially, including Action Plans.)

B. The Planning Council

This council will be a component of the "brain" of the program, part of the informal shadow government providing functions which don't exist now in any major institution in American society. It will specifically focus on the time perspectives (short-medium-long term) of policymaking and governance decisions and make plans for the nation (and future generations) as a collective. Those plans will emphasize major economic and social matters like environmental stewardship, employment development, economic progress, fiscal responsibility, funding of entitlement programs, and more. It will evaluate its topics with consideration of all temporal perspectives proposed and existing public policies for their compliance with the social ethos especially that of the *smart* governance concept. Like all of the councils, it will have a collective perspective and rationality and an emphasis on the application of reason, science, and technology solutions to social problems.

It will be populated by mostly experts specializing in time perspectives in a variety of fields. Many of the members will be volunteers from think tanks, universities, Big Business, and elsewhere having special intellectual and management skills (and good social character.) It will be both a policy/decision-making resource and an informal supervisor of sorts of legal government. Its enforcement will come from its credibility and its recommendations for Action Plans (of the Local Council, etc.) to compel legal government to act smart, even if some actors (e.g., the elite, Big Business elements, etc.) don't want to because mid-long-term consequences don't fit their business models, electoral cycles, or personal agendas. Too bad!

C. The Policy and Problem Solving Council

This Council will have a similar membership profile to the Planning Council but with more emphasis on problem-solving skills. That includes management of institutions, processes, and people. It also includes sophisticated understanding of how governments and citizens are motivated–partly by reason, but also by emotions, values, psychology, and habits.

The membership will be primarily comprised of academics and experts in a variety of fields organized into subdivisions targeting specific social problems and coordinated by a higher-level committee of nimble-minded supervisors with good judgment.

Its design characteristics include similar concepts involving collective perspective and fairness to those of the military base closings commissions of years past and the Simpson/Bowles budget reform committee of 2010. Unlike them, however, its tenure will be permanent, its jurisdiction much broader and more diverse, its approach more sophisticated and in harmony with the new set of public values, and hopefully, its profile having way more credibility. There are no other macro-level institutions in America now which will come close to its credibility profile of expertise, professionalism, collective perspective, and social character including, the Congress, the Executive Office, or any state governmental entities.

The Council will analyze, research, and design solutions to social issues like health care system improvement, effective alternatives to the simplistic war on drugs, comprehensive regulation of the financial industry, rationalization of the tax system, a comprehensive immigration policy, and similar matters. These are big projects and the Council may start out with smaller ones initially to build up competence and credibility with the public.

Like with the Planning Council, it's meant to take a *smart* approach to its mission. In this case, that means involving the perspective of all stakeholders; having multiple perspectives to all issues; being nonpartisan and non-biased; having nimble fair-minded personnel; applying reason, science, and technology-based design solutions to social problems; and addressing all of the levels of human experience (reason, emotions, values, psychology, and habit) which relate to any specific problem.

Furthermore, the collective fairness solutions will be premised on addressing *all* of the consequences to *everyone*. All parties affected by a solution in a negative way, for example, will be offered soft landing programs which would include, perhaps, advance notice of changes, provide for transitions, help in relocating capital and labor resources to new endeavors, compensations of sort for extraordinary losses, and others.

Since it will be made known early on that *all* segments of society will be subject to similar smartness changes nearly everyone will recognize the fairness of the disruption to *their* industries or social segment.

No one activity or group is being picked on, so to speak. This approach ought to gain the credibility of all those effected because the collective (of which everyone is a part) will benefit and the direct participants will have been treated fairly and gently. (Consider this approach with that of the Grand Reconciliation Project--see below.)

As one example of this approach consider the medical malpractice area. Our present system results in a small fraction of victims getting compensation, those who do suffer the convoluted litigation process, health professionals engage in wasteful and costly defense practices attempting to fend off potential claims, and the process ignores what most victims want from their professionals anyway which is truthful and apologetic responses, not merely the potential of monetary recovery.

From a smart approach perspective, the whole area is really an easy fix. Compensation of victims can be modeled after the workers compensation program, for example, where nearly all victims get recoveries without litigation, recovery amounts would be guided by expertly-designed compensation standards, health professionals would have less reason to be defensive thereby saving unnecessary efforts and costs, the many payment systems now would be reduced to one simple program, doctor-patient relationships would be improved, and overall costs to taxpayers and consumers likely lowered. Let's not forget the almost certain stress reductions for nearly everyone.

Health professionals in general will get substantial benefits even if perhaps a bit lower incomes. The stress reduction itself may be worth it. The plaintiff attorneys who bring malpractice suits would lose lucrative practices but would get a soft landing program allowing them to reorient themselves to different areas without fear of immediate and irreparable career losses. If that is not enough for them, too bad!

D. The Information Council

The individualist/capitalist system has sometimes subtle and unrecognized effects upon much of society beyond the economic aspects. The self-interested competitive ethos implicitly affects the sphere of public discourse where truth and respect for citizens and consumers is deprecated as they run counter to self-interest.

We all know well politicians' reputations for truth and respect for citizens! We all know well Big Business and the marketing industries' reputations for truth and respect of consumers! Like the intention involved in business transactions, the incentives in public discourse are to obtain advantages over others.

Truth and respect for citizens or consumers most often doesn't pay off. Those things may, for example, compromise the self-interest of a politician pushing for tax subsidies for a (favored) special interest which will allegedly "create jobs" to say truthfully that the public subsidies cost way more than the value of those jobs to the employees and the public. Big Pharmacy typically is loath to disclose secret research that its newest (highly expensive) drug is little better then generic or cheaper substitutes.

Individualism and competitiveness compel "litigation language," sort of like lawyers advocating for client positions. That kind of discourse provides only facts helpful to them, mischaracterizes ("spins") opponent facts and positions, and crafts deceptive "stories" to persuade judges and juries to favor their clients. As a matter of principle, *no one* active in the process has an interest in the Truth. And no one wants to respect the integrity of the audience (which has a moral right, at least, to full and honest information) for fear of compromising their own interests. Under the existing ethos, why should competitive parties have any interest in being truthful or respectful in any sort of public communications? If they try to be truthful and respectful, those who don't typically gain advantages. After all, misconceptions and manipulations are pretty effective.

Citizens and consumers of a smart society want and deserve better. One of this Council's primary functions will be to add Truth and Respect to the world of public discourse. Its specific functions will be:

-**News**: ensuring that credible news and journalism about matters important to citizens is available and accessible. It will develop accessible programs to honestly inform and educate citizens and consumers. It will counter lowbrow entertainment based "news" sources and it will turn news distribution and political discourse upside down meaning that it will creatively give people what they ought to have to be good citizens. Rather than pander to them or distract or numb them by entertainments so they don't recognize the possibilities that exist for major social change the Council will *empower* them. It will piggyback presentation of its agenda off of existing media sources or create its own, including a sophisticated computer interface providing news, information, and other matters important for the pushback efforts.

- **Information:** develop and maintain easily accessible information databases containing materials on economics, politics, social relations, and other similar matters important for citizens and consumers to be smart about their social lives. Some of the databases and educational programs will be specifically designed to inform the general public about the characteristics and positions of every major social group to inspire people to learn about other religions, cultures, and social positions. They will creatively demonstrate the commonality of social groups and facilitate the diminution of social frictions. Let's clearly explain to some, for example, what Islam and socialism are all about. Let's examine why the sharp cleavage between Red-Blue state is objectively invalid and deliberately stoked, in part, by those with self interested agendas, etc. (This material is part of the bridging function of the program—see Chapter 9 for details.).

-**Truth and Respect**: monitor campaign, political, Big Business lobbying, and marketing discourse and evaluate it for truth and respectfulness. The Council will expect a certain amount of full and fair disclosures about political policy proposals and consumer-related statements. That means analyzing the public statements of these parties which are designed to influence public opinion (for self-interested purposes) and determining whether they are factually accurate, partially true but misleading, fair characterizations, and/or in compliance with good social character standards. (This is a sort of a "Bullsh*t Translator" function.) If not, they will be rated according to a standard and Action Plans put into place to identify the miscreants for what they are, shame them, and/or counter any improper influences. For those truthful and respectful statements, proponents will be commended and/or rewarded.

-**Honorable Science:** The Council will counter, to some degree, the increasing proprietary aspect of scientific research. Big Business is eroding the credibility of the scientific enterprise itself by dominating its funding, findings distribution, and direction.

The Council will promote basic research for "knowledge" purposes not merely profit ones. It will sponsor Best Practice templates requiring all research findings to be published and accessible to everyone regardless of content or results. There will be conflict of interest and similar disclosures for all studies. It will sponsor research into those matters relevant to BMR and social relations which, for the most part, are not valuable to profit-making entities.

-**Spokesman Institution:** The Council will be a sort of go-to body for quality, credible news and information regarding public affairs. In essence, the information provided by this Council will be equivalent to "Everything that an intelligent/responsible citizen/consumer would want to know about matters of public discourse."

-Best Practice Templates

It will create templates of all kinds to raise the level of public discourse, increase the credibility of political and consumer discourse, and guide accessible governmental reports of various kinds. It will grade each major instance of public discourse against the set of of Best Practices templates and call out those which violate the standards. (Given the present standard of public discourse, the Bullsh*t Translator function may be very active!) The idea is to ensure that the audience gets Truth and all the material they need to participate well in the social world as well as being treated with respect. We don't want the big speakers to dictate to us what material they want us to act upon (i.e., be manipulated by.) We want them to provide to us what *we* need and want.

Here are some types of templates that the Council may promote:

Governmental

-accessible financial cash flow and net worth statements with schedules for debt, tax revenues by class, etc.
-multinational comparisons for a variety of social elements like healthcare outcomes, the social happiness index, educational achievement, etc.
-1/5/10 (and more) year national plans for achieving full employment, debt reduction, peacemaking, and the like
-rational and collective standards for apportionment, campaigning, election, and other similar political world activities
-a universal set of ethics for public officials

Public political communications

-full disclosure and fair characterizations (i.e., No BS!) of policy positions, e.g., what a proposal intends to do, who benefits (or not), budgeting and employment implications, sponsorship, etc., all with comprehensiveness and without deception
-full funding disclosures for candidates, parties, and lobbyists
-standards of what is appropriate character evaluation for candidates. (Some elements of privacy and relevance, not honored now by the news media especially, need to be upheld.)

Science

-require scientific research to contain disclosures of things like—sources of funding and motivations? Conflicts of interest/bias by researchers/scholars? Etc.

-disclosure of research results of *all* studies not just those that support the self-interests of manufacturers, marketers, and profit-oriented enterprises

-Online access to raw data of all studies

Business and employment

-Expertly-determined compensation and benefits packages-templates across many private industries and sectors, nonprofit, and public positions allowing comparisons

-Baseline compensation packages for nearly all workers taking into consideration human needs and not necessarily system-only ones

-Expertly-defined forms for clarity and comprehensiveness in consumer transactions, like borrowing, buying, warranties, etc.

Social and environmental

-national/international standards of achievement for all students at all levels

-curricula containing elements of multiculturalism, humanism, harmonious social relations, and the like

-best practices in environmental behavior for business, government, and homeowners

-social group educational and experience guides and opportunities

-greater uniformity in laws, regulation, consumer affairs, health standards, etc. across states and other jurisdictions.

E. The Communications Council

The Council's main function is to design and run a digital communication network which will connect all of the institutions and individuals who participate in the program. The infrastructure will include communication applications; social media; access to databases, news and collaborative websites; and the all-important end user interface–the Dashboard. That interface will make it easy for nearly anyone to participate in some way with the program. It will have relevant news, action alerts, surveys, pushback tools of various sorts, and more. There may be other non-digital communications components to the network for program participants.

The Council will be populated primarily by technological gurus and Internet/social media mavens, some paid and other volunteers. The architecture of the network will respond to the top-down/bottom-up organic organizational process. National level councils will feed inputs into the system while those at the lower levels will respond and/or provide information going upwards.

F. The Support Council

This Council, among other things, will secure the personnel needed throughout the program. That includes establishing selection processes for National Council membership, engaging the experts and professionals for the other councils, and developing a large volunteer group.

In addition, it will:

-obtain funding
-perform as a *general interest* organization within the traditional political processes
-perform traditional electoral and political activities like lobbying and the like
-develop social conditioning programs for many aspects of the program
-develop the organizational infrastructure by consolidating existing activist groups creating the "nodes" connecting local entities
-administer the rewards programs
-act as a liaison with Big Business and legal government to the extent that those entities will cooperate with the program

G. The Local Council

This will be the heart and even the guts of the program. It is the entity which will have the leverage to provide the bulk of the pushback as it will mobilize the voting numbers and the consumer powers of multi-millions of activist organizations and Marys and Johns. These people will initially organize into local groups, be united into larger groups (including the professional activist organizations), and tie into the network being overseen by the National Councils.

Its primary function will be enforcing pushback, but it will have other functions also:

-inspiring the little people to help themselves while providing them tools to do so

-monitoring legal government and Big Business for compliance with BMR
-perform the pushback Action Plans
-build and enhance the social fabric
-represent the inclusivity theme and emphasizing the public citizen attitude social category

H. The Public Citizen University

The University will explore the new philosophical concepts of the movement including the shadow government, dual citizen attitudes, the human component to capitalism, the mixed private/public economic system, the *psychological* view of class divisions instead of economic ones, and the concept of an advanced 21st-Century society

It will set up an informal curricula of public citizen values education across existing institutions. Part of that curricula will be to develop new leadership and management types having *holistic* approaches to society and to social problem-solving. Developing leadership of this type will be the opposite of what the current system does which is to emphasize a narrow focus and a high degree of specialization.

It will also develop the bridging function types having specialized skills in breaking down trivial social group differences and incompatible, simplistic mindsets. These people will be experts at addressing people and issues at all levels of experience–reason, emotion, etc.

2. The National Conventions

The conventions will be a set of establishing meetings organized by movement supporters. They can happen at the top, middle, or even lowest levels, but it will be much better if high profile, Big Producer types at the top level set the stage for the movement. The social ethos has to be explained and promoted by influencer types to followers and constituents.

Another necessary component of the organization is an imprimatur of sorts of intellectuals and academics which will establish the soundness of the vision and the practicality of the plan (if not its likely success.)

Since the program requires no defined organization, it can grow organically from all directions. Managers of large scale, mostly volunteer organizations will have to come forward to bring the movement to life. Assuming the meetings establish the basic principles, other meetings can start developing the components–the technical infrastructure, the social media outputs, the template designs, the distribution of ideas to the public, strategies to promote the ideas and values, etc.

There will be two fundamental types of meetings – those regarding traditional organizing and management efforts and those directed to the substantive content. That content would include bridging strategies, designing the Planning and Policy and Problem-Solving Councils, determining what problems to address first and how, etc.

3. The Grand Reconciliation Project

This project is a more comprehensive variation of the substantive convention meetings noted above creating a collective frame of reference for matters of American governance and social relations. It will be designed to get representatives of all major groups and positions in society with different interests, positions, and mindsets together and to attempt to reconcile them into a meta--level collective (American-nation) interest. That reconciliation would become a large part of a new social constitution.

Grand Reconciliation Project

Meetings and Resolutions

trivial discriminations
- race
- gender
- sexual orientation
- other

-role of religion in public affairs
- jurisdictions
- relationship overlaps

capital and labor
- allocations and relationships
- labor rights
- managerial rights and prerogatives

governmental affairs
- ethics
- compensation
- jurisdictions and efficiencies
- tax policy
- welfare state/ public services

democratic processes
- elections, etc.
- campaign financing
- terms of office
- ethics
- compensation
- communications

foreign affairs
-aid
-limitation of war powers
-military state

New Magna Carta-like Proposals

- public information, hearings, etc.
- referendum
- legitimization
- implementation and legalization–gradual and deliberative

The participants, even though representing their own group interest and positions, would nevertheless be selected as fair and nimble minded, empathetic (or helped to be so), having a good faith belief in bringing Americans together in a collective perspective, creative, and patient enough to make major social reframing possible.

There are historical models of people coming together into rational common enterprises. The United Nations and the European Union are major examples. Comprehensive international trade and business treaties are a lesser but still instructive set of examples. What we want to do with the program is way more ambitious but there are good reasons to think that the time is here to remake our ways of governance and social relations. A 21st-Century social constitutional convention may be the way to get started.

Every class, faction, group, perspective, etc. participating in the conferences will be treated fairly in the new social constitution. Fair-minded people will likely accept reinterpretations, meta-perspectives, sacrifices, and a reordering of rewards, incentives, and positions as long as everyone is treated fairly and with justification. We will try to put everyone into a Rawlsian-view position and ask them to assess Project proposals with the "veil of ignorance" implied by that concept. Assuming we can get everyone to see eye-to-eye at the abstract level then we use strategies to bridge the gap to our current realities. That will take time as everyone has vested positions which may have to be upended. But, fair-minded people who have witnessed generations and centuries of wars, hatred, and inhumanity, even though the elements of a more positive life are apparent especially now, will eventually learn to get along (with some difficulties, of course.)

The Grand Reconciliation will be a start. In a metaphorical sense, we put all of the relevant parties together in a large room, let everyone stomp around and vent about the others, let the heat dissipate, and then cool-headedly bang out a compromise about everyone's place and role in the newly conceived society. Nearly everyone will need to adapt to new frames and multiple perspectives. They will have to break old habits and form new, better ones.

Not everyone, likely, will be very happy, but everyone will know that they have been *treated fairly* and that the compromise makes good sense for the *collective* (meaning *everyone* will benefit to some degree, at least.)

Summary–Chapter 9: The Story: End of Part 1-What's Next?

Completing the Story

This book has introduced the main characters–private and public citizens, described a social milieu–the individualist/capitalist ethos, and provided a bit of the back story of 200+ years of elite dominance and the failed attempts to end it. It itemizes what the lower classes need in a new, advanced society. It explains why the elements are present *now* for the little people to rewrite the story they are living with the help of a theoretically sound vision and a practical plan.

This chapter is about completing the story. That requires *you* readers to advance the narratives, fill in the details, and write a happy ending. This chapter states what has to be done, by whom, when, and how long it will take.

What we aren't sure of is the existence of the will of Americans to undertake the hard work required for major, permanent social change and the patience to wait for the program elements to mature. But, it is certain that *we* can either write our own story or continue to or allow the elite to have one for us. We already know what that is like!

A. What Has To Be Done?

1. Distribute the ideas to academics and public intellectuals for their assessment of its validity and feasibility. Convince Big Influencers and cue-givers at all levels who may support the movement to become early sponsors and to spread the ideas to their followers and cue-takers. We need leaders of progressive organizations to adapt the ideas for themselves and spread them among like-minded others. We can release copies of the book on the Internet and social media sites to generate attention from the general public. The materials will be made available free of charge covered by a Creative Common License.

2. Educate, collaborate, and revise. We either rely on supportive geeks and communication expert volunteers to start the digital infrastructure or engage professionals to do it. Here we want to educate and inspire the public, engage them in collaboration, revise the theory and plan as necessary, and build a buzz, as they say, to resonate among the public about a new social movement. This book is simply a Version 1.0 and a sketch and there will be additional minds who can offer important input to improve and extend it.

3. Build the Brand: The program needs a unique identity. It has to offer a simple storyline of the little guys pushing back on the elite. That means focusing on just the major values of BMR and smart governance, at least at the beginning. We need to convince existing organizations and activists to buy into the leverage concept—the need to consolidate (or at least coordinate) under the single brand. We need a *single* focus and accessibility to make it *easy* for everyone to understand and participate. We can eventually establish a mental "trigger," so to speak, which will bring BMR to mind in most aspects of daily life for most people, make attention to BMR become an every day *habit*, and have the Local Council network continuously accessible for everyone, for purposes of pushback.

The Brand equals: a focus on basic values, a single consolidated organization (the Big Voice), and accessibility for everyone. The little people will develop a class consciousness of sorts, develop an *attitude of entitlement* to BMR, and learn to push back against the existing ethos in nearly every aspect of their daily lives, assisted by the network and the digital Dashboard.

Ordinary Marys and Johns will be made attentive to these things:

-the difference between Me People (private citizens) and We People (public citizens)
-the general public can and will insist upon a balance of private and public interests
-human meanings are going to be required to be accepted by the economic system whether it likes it or not
-there will be respect for good social character and living the small life well, with rewards
-everyone should have pride in themselves regardless of social status; being the best that one can be is the new standard of success
-a brainless, anti-collective governance system will no longer be tolerated

4. Build Out The Best Practices Templates

Although the program is fundamentally an *approach* to problem-solving and not content-oriented, it *will* produce content in the form of planning, problem-solutions, and best practices templates. The templates will cover a range of matters from political campaigning and elections; owner-employee relationships; business-consumer relationships; "How to be a Good Parent, Neighbor, and Voter," etc.; and more.

The templates will be professionally designed guides of decision-making and behaviors. The idea is to make it *easy* for people to be Good Citizens, Parents, Businessmen, and the like. In an environment of constant demands, complexity, and insufficient time to get things done (much less done well), most people just might embrace help like this. You can call it "Nanny State" stuff but a better way of thinking of it is extended, continuous, social conditioning and cue-giving, like that of parents, coaches, teachers, bosses, etc. If after turning 18 years old someone considers himself to be fully mature and responsible and capable of consistent success in our world without help he is delusional!

Keep in mind that the templates are drawn from the perspective of the collective interest (something foreign to American culture), not like the many proprietary guides to behaviors for self-interested activities.

5. Build out the Big Voice

For generations, hundreds and thousands of progressive activists of all kinds have worked very hard on all kinds of progressive issues. They have combated Big Business, those with short-term perspectives and ignorant mindsets, and even "dumb" governments. There have been some successes, of course, but for the most part they have not pushed back the dominant individualist/capitalist ethos much at all. The enemy, so to speak, has remained mostly unaffected. Those efforts at changing the status quo by those separate groups pursuing separate issues are like mere pinpricks and have been comfortably ignored or marginalized by the elite.

Not only that, these efforts have failed to inspire and mobilize exactly what those activists need to deliver effective blows from a "Big Stick" upon the elite. That requires the focused involvement of millions of the little people. These well-meaning, hard working groups are mostly distinct entities with different focuses and goals, competing for the same limited resources, striving for attention of the public among thousands of others, and making it *impossible* for the little people to comprehend all of the activity much less be mobilized by it.

That mobilization is *absolutely key* to push back. We have to make it *easy* for people to participate. To repeat, that means a single brand with a simple, direct set of values and goals, a single organization (at least as the separate groups interface with the Brand), and an accessible way for everyone to participate as they see fit.

All of that becomes the Big Voice for mobilization and the Big Stick for pushback!

Our bridgers and node builders will help to make this happen by consolidating and/or coordinating organizations, focusing efforts and spending limited money more efficiently, and finding niches in the movement for all activists. That formulation will be coordinated by the National Council and the Support Council.

6. Start the National Conventions and the Grand Reconciliation Project

The movement will want to develop credibility right away. For one, that means developing formal structures and processes as it will become a big organization which requires management. That organization will do these things:

-establish a formal presence upon which all other aspects can build upon
-be a visible representative of the new social movement
-represent the fundamental principles and goals of the movement
-demonstrate the weightiness of the movement as the organization grows and matures
-develop credibility for the endeavor
-start defining the new social category of public citizen (versus private citizen)
-demonstrate the inclusivity theme of the program by uniting all kinds of people with varying interests, skills, and intentions under a common good perspective

The national conventions will be early meetings of people who support the movement. They will likely be organized by those with production, management, and Big Project experience. They will recruit other similar people and delegate tasks so that, eventually, the program starts to look like a serious movement.

The conventions will have both process and content meetings. Process meetings will be for the formal structure and operations. Content meetings will be about specific planning, problem-solving, and social conditioning projects. Each type will be populated with a different set of people–management and organizational types for the former and experts and content professionals for the latter (e.g., academics, substantive experts, etc.)

There will be a separate organizational process for the Grand Reconciliation Project. That can be expected to be a longer, more contentious endeavor. It requires a different set of people–representing all of the major identity and position groups in America. There hopefully will be a set of fair-minded, empathetic, rational folks acting in good faith to see social themes in new ways and reframe what we have. They could accomplish Great Things! Having a distinguished, diverse set of Great Americans come up with a new social constitution would be a major event and become a historical one if they can convince (by a variety of strategies) their followers to accept it. The movement will be a systemwide paradigmatic change not unlike the upsetting of the monarchy in the 18th-Century, the expansion of federal jurisdiction in America in the 1930's to 1970's, and the (mostly) successful race, gender, and sexual orientation rights movements.

It will take charismatic and persuasive people to organize a set of members of groups used to combating each other. Is it foolhardy *or* reasonable to expect to convince representatives of every major identity and interest group to want to rise above the 18th-Century ideas which now frame our governance and social relations and come up with something new? That's where the bridging people will be most active (see below.) Sometimes new ideas make so much sense that they can't be ignored. It could be that only the hard-core partisans and rigid-minded would object to the intentions.

The new social constitution which could develop out of this project will highlight a collective perspective, Rawlsian fairness, a new level of social trust, and moral and practical credibility. It will be a new (21st - Century new) and very different approach and require millions of people to re-reorient how they see and think about major social issues.

7. Create the National Councils

a. A preliminary National Council can be set up once the program has some momentum. There will be a quick, initial nomination and selection process set up by the Support Council replaced later by a nationwide process involving the general public. Some potential candidates would include people who have the high profile, good social character, macro-level experience, professional visions, and collective perspectives on the order of Jimmy Carter, futurist Ray Kurzweil, news columnist David Brooks, Barack Obama, Pope Francis, Warren Buffett, and similar others. (We don't necessarily want mostly "old guard" people but those with the right characteristics.)

b. The Communication Council ought to be set up early on to build the digital infrastructure and collaboration tools.

c. The Local Council can be built out mostly from the bottom up, likely by consolidation and/or coordination of existing progressive groups and new organizations of all kinds at the grassroots level, with the assistance of node builders.

d. The Support Council can be built out in phases. It has a lot of functions but will start out organizing volunteers and obtaining funding.

e. The Information Council can be built out in phases, too. It will have the largest set of functions and some of the more complicated ones.

f. The Policy and Problem-Solving Council can start developing its own infrastructure which may require not too much more than a network *overlay* over existing intellectual and professional resources, like think tanks, academics in university departments, and similar sources. A coordinating committee will guide its development, selection of projects, and manage the content teams to get them started, at least.

In order for it to actually solve problems this Council is going to have to earn some credibility first. But, at a minimum, it can start designing preliminary white paper and/or blueprints designs of problem-solving projects while keeping them in hand until society is ready for it to act. Since it has no formal authority itself it will have to advise with legal government, coordinate with major social institutions, and earn the support of the public. Like with most of the movement, the Council may have to *impose* itself upon supporters of the existing system utilizing pushback techniques.

g. The Planning Council development will be similar to the Policy and Problem-Solving Council, for most of the same reasons. Reaching an implementation phase may take longer as it will need the others in place for it to incorporate its functions with theirs.

h. The National University is not a priority as its functions are medium to long-term in any case. It may develop an academic program early on and get it institutionalized but it will take time to develop the curriculum, leaders, and managers we expect and even longer for the graduates to become effectively absorbed in social roles.

8. Amending the U.S. Constitution

This is a medium to long term project. Firstly, we will have to have our own legal experts carefully design the specific amendments being sure to keep their expected consequences limited only to what is necessary to implement the program's goals. We don't want to add content provisions as that will be beyond what the program stands for–smartness in *approach*–not specific new rights, etc. Good outcomes, however, ought to derive from a good approach. Secondly, we can't let this process become a free-for-all where special interests, political partisans, and even well-meaning public citizens attempt to load up the amendment process and eventually stymie the whole attempt.

-Here are some of the amendments of the Constitution we might propose:

-Article 1–extend terms of office; decrease the relative ratio of House Representatives to citizens; rework the proportional scheme in the Senate to reflect modern population realities and democratic ideals

-Article 1 of the Bill of Rights – rework the free speech provisions to allow campaign and elections reforms to minimize the ability of the elite to dominate discourse in the public sphere and its influence upon elections and the political processes

- Article 4 of the Bill of Rights–update privacy rights in the Internet Age. (This *is* a substantive provision but fits in well timewise with the amendment process and implies smartness and fairness issues.)

-Article 17—rework the Senate proportionality provisions.

B. The Right Characters

These are the categories of people the movement needs to proceed and succeed.

1. Executive producer-types and a "conductor," so to speak, to act like a committee chair to keep a clear direction going and coordinate everyone else. These people will be high-level organizers and leaders sort of like those who made up the Founding Fathers of the American nation in the 18th-Century. Some of them may be Big Ego types who know how to run big institutions, solve problems, and otherwise get things done. However, we don't want people with personal agendas, only those with the requisite good-faith intentions and good social character.

These will be some of their functions:

-organize the national conventions
-set up the Grand Reconciliation Project
-recruit high-level program managers for all of the councils
-develop a public relations program to build the brand
-set up nomination procedures for the National Council and other high-level positions
-coordinate the development of the program at all levels, top-down, bottom-up
-obtain funding

2. Symbolic, Emotional, And Spiritual Leaders. These will be high profile and prominent people in the media and popular culture, the communities, churches, and organizations of many types who can appeal to the values, emotions, and psychology of the public and their membership as cue-givers. They will focus simply on BMR and smartness in governance. For the most part, the appeal to the values of their audiences may be the most meaningful in garnering their support and even participation. (The *opportunities* for participation will be made available from other sources.)

3. Public relations and marketers. These people will have a similar function to the symbolic, emotional, and spirituality leaders except that they will focus on the general public. The program is primarily about seeing and thinking about social issues in new ways and these folks are experts at conditioning mindsets in the public. If they can get consumers to buy everything from the most overpriced, worthless products and services and get them to support the least-qualified political candidates they should be able to get them to buy into new social categories like Me People/We People and BMR. We want to create categories that resonate well with the public sort of like the Occupy Wall Street idea of 1% versus the 99%'s, but with more validity and connected to a workable plan of change.

All of this will require multi-level approaches to how people experience social themes–reason, emotion, etc. It will also require multimedia strategies involving symbols, role models, and the like.

4. Content developers.

We can presume that there are out there plenty of smart people in all of the social science fields and plenty of skilled and experienced people running large businesses and organizations. There are already good quality plans, proposals, and strategies to deal with some of our major social problems, most of them denigrated by opposed special interests and the profit-oriented, and ignored by public officials having their own agendas. Some of them may not be suitable for implementation given the "dumb" governance architecture we have now.

Many of these people can get the attention they deserve, the quality ideas resurrected, and new people and ideas given opportunity to be creative and effective if the social ethos we promote comes into being. The logic is powerful that a smart governance architecture can support problem-solving solutions our 18th-century institutions cannot. It is likely that many public-oriented experts and problem-solving people, including newly inspired and energized little people, will volunteer (under the program auspices) to help remake America.

5. Managers, administrators, and support personnel.

Of course, like nearly all organizations, the program will require those with traditional managerial, administrative, and support skills. Some of these people may be employees of the program and some volunteers.

6. Local activists.

There is no shortage of committed, hard-working people with heart intending to reform/fix what they see wrong with America. Some, truthfully, may be misguided and without balance or perspective. Some are overzealous. The biggest problem, however is that they are doing their own things separately, without focus, or coordination. Each has minimal to no leverage and the result has been a meager set of mostly insignificant reforms to the system. The Big Guys still dominate and are more irritated by these people than threatened!

7. Node builders.

These people will be specialists in obtaining the consolidation, coordination, and bridging of those activists noted above and ordinary folks. They will bridge substantive issues and organizational differences, find niches for everyone, manage limited resources efficiently, and help make the Big Voice.

8. Computer geeks, Internet gurus, and social media mavens.

It's the new technology and access to information which makes the plan feasible. That's where the digital infrastructure fits in. We will engage professional network specialists as necessary to build out our network but there may be thousands or more volunteers who may be willing to contribute, especially those still in tune with the original spirit of Internet development.

Between the federal government's DARPA program in the 1970's and the legions of common good-oriented geeks who build out most of the original Internet, you have a large set of folks that may be thought of as the the original "digital socialists." Their motivations were practical applications of new science useful for themselves and any other interested parties. They believed that good science and technology belonged to the general public. They were mostly volunteers and non-profit oriented.

Much of the Internet today is maintained and developed by people with much of the same spirit, especially in the form of the Open Source movement. Careful readers will see a great deal of the program as borrowing a number of elements of the Open Source movement. Take for instance, the common good intentions; rationality; organic development; combined top-down and bottom-up organizational processes; design approaches like modular construction, scalability, shared templates (not code, but similar); continuous improvements; and more.

Having volunteer geeks like these take responsibility for the digital infrastructure and information accessibility seems like a natural development. The new technology future together with the political/ economic vision is a sort of *open source social change movement*. Even some of the politics of the program harmonize in good measure with the libertarian streak of many geeks.

Regardless, some geeks even may see the program's network as a technological challenge and want to get involved to solve the unique communication issues, while satisfying some of their own political wants.

9. Fundraisers and volunteer coordinators.

These are traditional roles, too, and essential components of nearly any organization. Getting participation in any volunteer organization is almost always difficult but the program will have roles as small as merely clicking on a few icons on one's own computer every so often. That may not be overly demanding for most, especially when they recognize the benefits of being part of the American Team.

10. Lobbyists and political operatives.

The program is not going to replace our existing political processes only complement them in sophisticated ways. That means we would be wise to participate in those traditional processes in order to influence them using our new leverage. Our people will do policymaking, lobbying, and the like but only on the basis of a *general interest* approach and in coordination with the program processes overall. We also will scrupulously not be part of any of the traditional "immoral" activities of typical special interests involved in the political sphere.

11. Bridgers.

Bridging has hardly been a notable concept in American history. Generally, Americans consider themselves as free-minded individualists with a powerful sense of personal autonomy. While some of that attitude is justified, too much of it (as we have now in 21st-Century America) leads to persistent competition and conflicts. It's primitive, jungle-like stuff greatly out of place in a predominantly urban, highly interconnected society (and globe.)

The social characteristics most relevant now include empathy, multiple perspectives, tolerance, cooperation, and a collective consciousness. The persistent "us versus them" mindsets which seem to apply nearly everywhere (some deliberately stoked by partisans for personal agendas) ought to give way to the collective American Team idea. Bridgers will be people who have the right character and the charisma to bring people together. They will target those group leaders who benefit from divisiveness and try to reform them, or find a process to replace them if necessary with more modern, tolerant leaders.

Bridging will take a lot of forms including social conditioning programs for educational and "other party" experiences, building neighborhood and regional associations, toning down cultural provocations, and more.

12. Monitors.

These people will be part of the Local Council and the shadow government. They will specialize in keeping governments, public officials, and Big Business in compliance with the laws and our new ethics codes. They will report violations to one of the Councils for remedy–Action Plans, for example.

The means may be not much more than monitoring news and databases even from home computers connected to the network. Some of the more righteous Tea Party members may be well-suited for this role.

13. Public Citizens.

Public citizens will bring their *attitude of entitlement* to BMR and smart governance to pushback in many aspects of their daily lives. That may mean in the workplace, relating to consumer transactions, within the political processes, and other ways. They will learn to recognize a "trigger" to remind them them to assert BMR and to engage the Local Council to implement Action Plans, as necessary.

Given the class demographics of American society we won't need much more than 15-30% of Americans to be attentive to the program.

14. Critics and naysayers.

Much of the elite class will be opposed, of course, to any part of the movement. We already have discussed how to deal with that (i.e., pushback.) There also will be serious critics and naysayers who may find flaws and problems with the program. A grand movement like described here, and only a sketch of one, is certainly going to need continued work. We will listen to them and fix what needs to be fixed. We will actively seek that kind of critique as that is smart, too. The fundamentalists and the small set of chronic moaners and groaners will have to be marginalized or ignored.

C. What Do We Do Right Now?

Probably the program has to get some traction with at least a small set of important opinion leaders and cue-givers first before much else can happen. That may occur after it has been distributed to some of those types and released on the Internet via social media sites and the like.

The program really is primarily a top-down first project. But people in the following groups may get involved in various ways early on, at least tentatively. It is conceivable that the movement could build out from any level, organically, especially by the activist groups and progressives, the large unions, and by college-level youths.

1. Activists and progressives

It is likely that most of the existing activist groups will chafe at the program's key elements of the new social categories—We/Me People, the need for the single brand, the deliberate focus on BMR, and others. Not many people like change, especially to theories and methods that they have committed to for years.

However, this is a new paradigm after all and all of that resistance is expected. Nevertheless, until enough of these folks come to realize that the old ways don't work and become willing to try something new and different the program will not work like it should. The reality is that these groups can do pretty much what they are doing now but under the auspices of the brand. In accepting the key strategies of focus,

What's Next?

A. What Has To Be Done?

-Distribute the Ideas

-Educate, Collaborate, and Revise

-Build the Brand

-Build out the Best Practices Templates

-Build out the Big Voice

-Start the National Conventions and the Grand Reconciliation Project

-Create the Councils

-Amend the U.S. Constitution

B. The Right Characters

-Executive Producer Types

-A "Conductor"

-Symbolic, Emotional, and Spiritual Leaders

-Public Relations and Marketers

(Cont'd.)

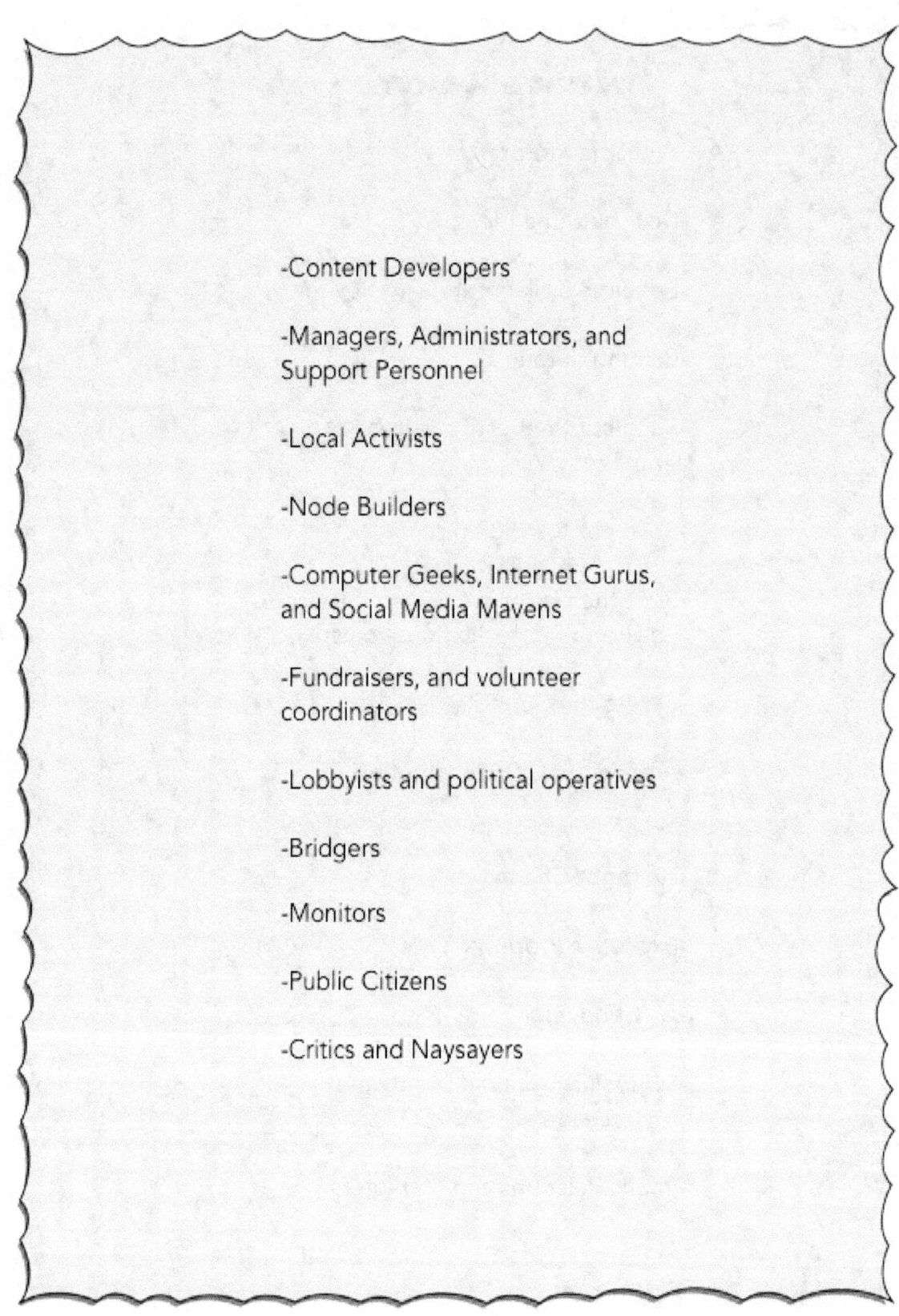

-Content Developers

-Managers, Administrators, and
Support Personnel

-Local Activists

-Node Builders

-Computer Geeks, Internet Gurus,
and Social Media Mavens

-Fundraisers, and volunteer
coordinators

-Lobbyists and political operatives

-Bridgers

-Monitors

-Public Citizens

-Critics and Naysayers

C. What Do We Do Right Now?

-<u>Activists and progressives</u> —form local coalitions, refocus on BMR and smart governance, and find a niche in the Brand.

-<u>Big Business (& Small)</u> —Adopt BMR principles in the workplace, industries and the environment

-<u>Unions</u>— Reformulate into general interest organizations

-<u>Non-union; non-professionals</u>— pressure informally by relying on templates

-<u>Professionals</u>—drawn upon the templates to obtain BMR

-<u>Governments</u>— not much

-<u>Politicians & Governmental Officials</u> Adapt the social ethos to the extent possible from the inside

-<u>The Elite</u>—Get on the right side of the movement early; make opportunities to become program leaders

-<u>Bridgers & Node-builders</u>—Propose plans to unify activist groups; propose strategies to unify   (Cont'd.)

<u>Activists on the Right</u>—Reformulate your theory and practices to the new private/public concepts; Adopt BMR principles and join the Big Voice

<u>College Kids & Youths</u>— Help create the new social movement on campuses and elsewhere. Pressure campuses and employers to adapt to BMR.

<u>Minority Cultures</u>—Lesser identity and positions groups & continue with other activist into the America Team.

<u>Mary's and John's</u>—Develop an attitude of entitlement to BMR. Assert it in the workplace, consumer world, and political sphere.

D. How Long Will It Take?

No one knows.

But, getting the ethos started — 2-3 years? Getting the structures going— 4-8 years? Implementing the entire program — two generations?

unity, accessibility, and credibility they can find their own niches and work with others. Most significantly, they will have a serious chance of *real* success!

While these groups can start making some adjustments now, in the nature of forming local coalitions, refocusing towards BMR principles, and the like, the bulk of the effort will likely have to wait until high profile credibility from the top of the program starts to happen. The basics have to be established first and the brand has to develop some recognition. After that point a comprehensive needs chart will be created to guide people to how they can fit in.

2. Big Businesses (and small)

In some respects, parts of the social ethos we are trying to affect are already influencing aspects of Big Business. For example, many businesses are becoming legal B-Corporations and otherwise balancing profit-making with social good. Many are taking ownership of their social presences by being environmentally conscious, controlling externalities, influencing their suppliers to do the same, and even addressing the economic and social concerns of (of all people!) ordinary workers! That includes raising compensation levels, flexing job schedules, etc.

A wide-spread social ethos may move entire industries and many businesses to adapt to BMR principles, especially if the competitive angle is minimized by (near) universal compliances. Businesses which sincerely adjust will likely be rewarded by customer loyalty and social rewards of various kinds. Those that don't may be on the wrong side of the fence, so to speak, and either wither or defiantly attempt to weather the new social pressures.

3. Unions

If the unions don't clean up their acts, so to speak, the biggest component of pushback will be missing. The movement may be fatally wounded if we can't push back on the crucial capital/labor value ratio. Influencing mindsets alone will not be sufficient. That means compelling reluctant owners/managers to give up what they want to retain most–money. The unions will have the most and best resources to do that.

The unions have to become reformulated first. That means becoming *general* interests; having a collective perspective acknowledging the interest of all stakeholders; forsaking overreaching; and reforming internally to eliminate excessive hierarchies, "bossism," criminal influences; utilizing best practice templates in the workplace; accepting designed templates for compensation schemes; and enacting an extensive public relations effort to convince the public that all of those things above now are true.

4. Non-union, non-professional workers

These people have little leverage and will rely mostly on outside help. That includes statutory assistance for enhanced compensation and benefits and workplace influence. They also can rely on templates created by the program to put informal pressures upon management to act regarding best practices. They may have to wait, mostly, for that outside assistance to come into play but courageous supporters can start to assert BMR at any time.

5. Professionals

While these people have more influence in the workplace, including having formal support for things like work-life balance, the reality is that most of them are just as much wage slaves as the ordinary Marys and

Johns. However, once the program develops, its ethos may eventually seep into the workplace giving these folks "cover," so to speak, to insist upon those changes important to them.

6. Governments

For the most part, governments are not going to adapt much on their own. There have been a few efforts resulting in minor inside adjustments like the California Thinking Long Project. Governments, however, have institutional and legal constraints and generations of habits. They will have to be changed from the outside.

7. Politicians and governmental officers

Again, individuals already in the political sphere who may support BMR and smart governance are constrained by the same factors noted above. They will have to rely on reforms imposed from the outside. That doesn't mean they can't support the program informally from the inside in conjunction with outside pressures. That means attempting to increase professionalism, competence, ethics, and the like, at least tentatively, until more formal templates are available.

8. The elite

Most of the elite will be opposed to the program. They want to *enhance* private interest, not constrain it. On the other hand, many elite members like Warren Buffett, Starbucks' Howard Schultz, and others recognize the economic injustices and favor reforms of various sorts. (We will insist upon more than just that, but at least we will have some supporters among the elite.)

Supportive elite members can endorse the program at the top level, adapt the program principles to their own businesses and institutions, become symbolic leaders, and cue-givers. They can take formal leadership positions in the national conventions and national councils, especially, and grasp leadership opportunities to become social heroes akin to those of the civil rights and feminist eras.

9. Bridgers and node builders

Until the top-down level principles are established these people will not have the brand concept to help them organize the middle layers of activist groups. Nevertheless, they can still start plans to create the Big Voice network, create templates, and get separate organizations to develop coordination among themselves, at least.

10. Activists on the right

True Classical Conservatives might support smartness and more professional governance, the emphasis on public values, the raising of public performance by social conditioning, and even some of the pushback as long as it leaves the elite primary influence in steering the "Ship of State,"—(the little people will *never* earn that right, in their view.)

The economic component of the Tea Party and the Occupy Wall Street folks have a large overlap in their goals. They know that they have been screwed and are fighting back. This program gives them both a theoretical vision of who/what is responsible and how. It gives them a feasible plan to remedy some of their problems. Occupy can renew its efforts now with a vision and plan. They can push the essential concepts of BMR and smart governance from the middle level. That will give them the effectiveness they haven't had. The Tea Party can refocus on a new target—the private citizen elite.

Those on the "right" will favor the emphasis on public values and should not oppose smartness and more professional governance. If they can be flexible enough, they will adapt to the new social categories of private and public and give up their identity and group ones. They could embrace BMR as the right way to approach class relations. They can become a useful part of the Big Voice.

Fundamentalists will be outraged, of course, and obstructionist.

11. College kids and young people

 Younger generations now are more likely to lack hope than previous ones, with good reasons. This program, like most social change movements throughout history, will rely heavily on youthful energy and creativity. This program truly offers them hope and way more. The expected mid-long-term benefits will reach them first. A unique historical opportunity to do great things may be enticing. They can create buzz about the new social movement on campuses, try to implement BMR in their schools and youth groups, and perhaps carry that over to their employment situations.

There may be a seed of a 21st-Century counterculture here.

12. Minority cultures

Being brought into a grand social movement like this ought to be special for these groups. If anyone should push for BMR it ought to be them. They can start by inspiring their identity communities to buy into the collective principles while forging bonds with the other little people as a new group. They can try to create bridges which will bring them into the American Team, as "regular" people instead of as identity-based ones.

13. Marys and Johns

Provided the social ethos develops from the top down and gets delivered to the general public by high-profile endorsers and cue-givers the ordinary Marys and Johns will learn an attitude of entitlement to BMR. The principles are simple enough, the middle-layer of the program will coalesce and provide focus, and the network will provide accessibility. That attitude can be expressed readily everywhere in daily life. They are not going to "take it anymore!" They will insist upon constraint of private interests, demand consideration for their humanity, and insist upon respect for living the small life well, at work, the political sphere, and in the consumer world.

D. How Long Will It Take?

No one knows. No one knows if anything at all will develop. You readers will have a say in that.

There will be short, medium, and long term durations for different aspects of the program's development. Perhaps, making the social ethos a part of public discourse could take two to three years. The structural development could take four to eight years. The implementation of everything else may take a couple generations. However, when the little people have been dominated for centuries working for peanuts, working for major social change only for a couple generations should feel like nothing.

About the Author

Why is the author here listed as anonymous-(New Ideas)?

He is a very private person who prefers the low-profile. He believes the ideas presented here ought to stand on their own and personal identification would just get in the way of attention to those ideas.

There is not much interesting about him in any case except for these facts:

1. He is one of the little people. He has always felt bad that so many hard working, high quality little people living the small life well so often get beat up in the political economy without *good* reason.

2. He truly believes that the National Character Program is a sound vision and plan to change their status in society.

3. He feels an existential urge to add what *he* can to that goal.

4. Beyond the moral imperative, the author has credentials. He has a Phd. in Political Science from a national university and concentrated on "grand theory." He also has a JD and has been an attentive observer of social science topics like economics, politics, and social relations nearly all of his life.

'Nuff said?   (www.theactionmanual.com)

Covers graphics by:Daniel Ryves

Contacts and Information

1. The National Character Program maintains a **website** at: www/theactionmanual.com

2. A **blog** with open commentaries is accessible at: www/theactionmanual.com/the-blog

3. The **Twitter feed** is at: @theactionalmanual

4. **E-mails** are received at: author@theactionmanual.com

5. **Financial contributions** can be made to the National Character Program at the website at:

    www.theactionmanual.com/contacts

6. **Paperback versions** of this book can be purchased at: www.Amazon.com